ADVANCED RUT HUNTING

Strategies for Taking Whitetails
During Prime Time

Edited by GERALD BETHGE

The Lyons Press
Guilford, CT
An Imprint of The Globe Pequot Press

The Lyons Press is an imprint of The Globe Pequot Press

10 9 8 7 6 5 4 3 2 1

Designed by Compset, Inc.

10 9 8 7 6 5 4 3 2 1

Library of Congress Cataloging-in-Publication data

Advanced rut hunting / edited by Gerald Bethge.

     p. cm.

  ISBN 1-59228-102-8 (pob : alk. paper)

  1.   Deer Hunting. 2. Deer—Behavior. 3. Rut. I. Bethge, Gerald.

  SK301.A28 2003

  799.2'7652—dc21

                        2003009450

CONTENTS

Contents

INTRODUCTION

I was probably fifteen or so when I first heard about a whitetail deer hunting tactic that promised to be so revolutionary that it would change the way sportsmen hunt deer forever. I don't recall who wrote the story or even in what magazine I had seen it, yet I can vividly recall reading it so many times that the ink faded from the pages. It concerned the mysterious ritual that whitetail deer go through each fall called the rut. Back in the '70s, wildlife biologists were just beginning to learn about the sometimes-bizarre breeding behavior of whitetails. Scrapes, the author revealed, are where whitetail bucks and does advertise their presence to each other. His recommended hunting tactic was to find a scrape in the woods, set up a treestand or ground blind nearby, and wait for the buck to return. When he does, you've got him!

Now, I had seen "scrapes" in the woods for as long as I had been old enough to walk there, but I never had a clue as to what those bare-earth patches of ground were until I read that story. Armed with this incredible new information, I dutifully parked my butt near a scrape for two or three straight years during bow, firearms, and muzzle-loader season; during rain, sleet, and snow; and regardless of wind direction—and never even saw a doe, let alone Buckzilla. Matter of fact, I was convinced that none of the scrapes that I had set up on had ever been revisited by a buck. Back then, though, I was about as young and dumb as they came in the deer woods—strong in the enthusiasm department but not really swift tactically speaking. With a deer population holding firm at about two per square mile, the odds were firmly stacked against me. But I believed! Why? Because anything can happen during the rut—and it usually does.

Whitetail rut behavior and the hunting strategies resulting from our clearer understanding of it have come a long way since the

'70s. Biologists and outdoor writers have helped immeasurably in the process. We now know—almost to the exact date—when white-tails breed in a particular geographic region thanks to the back-dating of fawn fetuses. We can translate deer vocalizations and body language; have better knowledge of the size of a buck's home range; know that bucks make rubs to mark their territory and not to strip velvet from their racks; know they respond to calls and can be lured into range with scents; and much, much more.

Even with all this new knowledge, however, one aspect re-mains very much the same today as it was thirty and even forty years ago: The rut is the epitome of hope. The hope that the biggest buck in your deer woods will be so focused on his urge to mate that he'll finally make a mistake and saunter past within range of your gun or bow. It's what makes us wake up before dawn each day of the season in conditions that continually push us to the limits of our en-durance. The best part is that never have our chances of shooting a giant buck been better than they are right now. Thanks to factors like quality deer management programs, food plot management, and discriminating hunters, trophy bucks can come from virtually anywhere in the United States and Canada.

Remember that scrape I mentioned sitting over in my youth? Just a couple of seasons ago, another buck opened a scrape in that exact spot. Trail timers confirmed my suspicions, and with it the conclusions of many wildlife biologists. Situated along a field edge, the scrape had indeed been revisited, but only under the cover of darkness. My best chance to take the buck that made it, I surmised, was to wait for the peak of the rut's chase phase and hope for a day that promised to bring with it a drastic weather change. Does, out and about to feed before an approaching weather front, would hope-fully lure the buck out and into a place where I could get a shot at him with shooting light to spare. It worked to perfection—almost.

It was just the second day of shotgun deer season. The night before brought with it three or four inches of fresh snow. More bored than cold, I began to still-hunt my way from the scrape toward a nearby bedding area when a flash of movement caught my eye. With an antlerless deer permit in my pocket, I froze in my tracks and readied myself for a shot opportunity. Indeed, the flash of movement turned into a doe approaching at a rapid clip, but it was the glint of antler behind the doe that made my heart pound. Wild-eyed and with his nose to the ground, hound-dog-style, was the biggest whitetail buck I had ever seen in the wild. He was a thick-beamed, gnarly-horned giant with a palmated left antler beam.

I was caught completely flat-footed and out in the open, but the deer were oblivious. I shouldered the gun at seventy-five yards, drew a bead on the buck's chest at fifty, and squeezed off the first shot at forty-five. The doe jumped, stopped, looked my way, and then ran—closer! The buck paid no attention at all, nor did he topple over. I fired again, pumped the gun, and fired a third time. The buck never gave any indication that it was hit. Reaching into my pocket for shells, I reloaded and, with the two deer still within range, managed to empty the gun without cutting a hair. A final shell remained in my pocket. I reached for it and quietly reloaded the shotgun all the while watching the two deer. Their trotting semicircle path around me came to an end at just thirty-five yards. With the love-struck buck standing perfectly broadside, I took a deep breath, put the bead on his chest, and willed my final slug toward its target.

Impossibly, that buck calmly turned and trotted off into my memory (nightmares) forever. I was crushed. I sank to my knees and almost became physically ill. I followed the huge buck's tracks for a quarter-mile in the hope of finding him piled up somewhere, but after 100 yards it was clear that I had never touched him. In fact, the deer never even broke out of walking stride. The legend of "Teffie," the Teflon buck, was born that day. No one has seen so much as his shed antler since. It was almost as if he never existed, but I know he did and still might. Phantom bucks, like the rut itself, are all about faith and hope. What is hunting without them?

This book is an attempt to turn that faith into reality. We have asked the finest outdoor writers in the land to contribute to "Advanced Rut Hunting" and they've come through in spades. Inside these pages are some of the most enlightening tactics and strategies on successful rut hunting that have ever been published. Renowned deer experts Gary Clancy, Mike Hanback, John Weiss, Bob McNally, Peter Fiduccia, Bill Winke, Pat Durkin, Bill Vaznis, Dave Justmann, Curt Wells, Bob Robb, and Kenn Young have all come together in one place to help make you a better buck hunter this fall. Hey? Who knows? It might even help me get another crack at "Teffie."

—*Gerald Bethge*

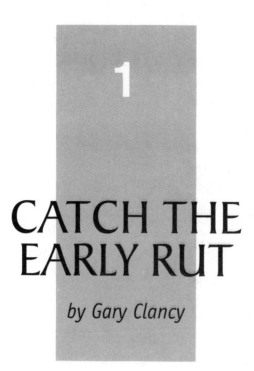

1

CATCH THE EARLY RUT

by Gary Clancy

Hunting the October mini-rut can give
you a jump on this year's bow season.

I've thought about writing on this topic for years, but have never had the guts to do it. You see, the subject is one that I can't support with reams of research or documentation. All I have to go on are my personal observations and those of other serious hunters. But I'm not just writing this article for the fun of it; I'm convinced that each October a "mini-rut" takes place that most hunters aren't aware of. This early rut provides a wonderful—if short-lived— opportunity for some great deer hunting action. I've seen breeding activity in mid-October too often during the past twenty years for it to be mere coincidence.

At first I simply dismissed these episodes as flukes. But when I began observing rutting behavior at about the same time each October, I began to wonder. What convinced me there was something going on was finally getting up the courage to tell some other serious hunters what I'd been seeing.

As a general rule, serious bowhunters tend to be a closed-mouth bunch. The best whitetail hunters aren't out to gain the approval of their peers. They just quietly go about the business of taking really good bucks every season. I'm fortunate to know a number of these archers, and when I began questioning them about the breeding activity I'd witnessed, most confessed that they'd been onto the early rut for a long time. Several simply gave me a sly smile and changed the subject. I guess I'm a slow learner.

In the coulee country of western Wisconsin near the Mississippi River, Tom Indrebo and his wife, Laurie, run an outfitting business called Bluff Country Outfitters. Tom doesn't have a degree in wildlife biology, but he knows as much about whitetail deer as any man I've ever met. The Indrebo's farm is whitetail central. Hunters and whitetail nuts are constantly dropping by to show Tom deer they've killed and sheds they've found, or just to swap stories. The Indrebos feed me and let me bunk down for the night when I'm hunting in the area.

On October 13, 1998, I showed up at their door an hour after dark and was ushered in to sit at the big table, where a half-dozen bowhunters and Tom were wolfing down roast beef and mashed potatoes. I ate and listened to the hunting stories; later, after the others had retired to their cabins, I told Tom what had happened to me that evening.

I described how I had gotten to my stand about 3 P.M. on a little flat where the white oaks were dropping acorns, and how a doe and twin fawns had shown up to eat an hour later. Nothing unusual there. But then a lone doe came hurrying down the ridge, and behind her I could hear a buck grunting. The doe skidded to a stop twenty yards from my stand, and I could tell she was an old gal because of her sway back and low-slung belly. The buck behind her turned out to be a scraggly seven-point, but he sure had big ideas. The old doe kept trying to eat, but the little buck kept slinking up on her, with his head low like he had certain intentions. The doe would scoot off, and the buck would stop and sniff where she had been standing. Once the doe urinated, and the buck put his nose down at that spot and curled his lip to catch the scent.

Before long another buck showed up, and then another. None of the three were what I was looking for, so I just sat back and enjoyed the show as the three took turns harassing the old doe. Just before dark a bigger buck—but still not the one I was looking for—joined in the game. As the last light was fading I saw the buck I'd been waiting for. I tried grunting him in, but there was so much grunting going on from the other bucks that he never paid any attention to me. None of the other bucks had scraped or rubbed the entire time, but the big buck made three scrapes within a few minutes and took time to work over a wrist-thick maple. It was too dark to shoot, so I just watched through binoculars. After the big buck finished with the maple, he walked stiff-legged toward the doe. The other bucks made room for him, and the doe walked off with the big boy's nose right on her tail.

"Now here is the real kicker, Tom," I finished. "Last year on October 12, I was sitting on that same flat, in the same tree, when virtually the same thing happened. What's going on?"

Indrebo kicked back in his chair, snared another cookie from the plate, and spent the next hour sharing similar experiences he and his guests have had each October. Summing up, he said, "I'm convinced that on about the same date each October a few of the

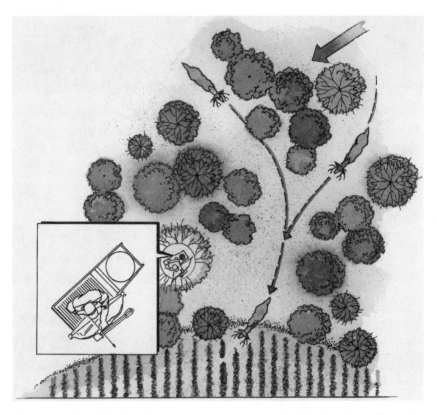

During a typical fall, the oldest, most mature does will come into heat first, often attracting a host of prospective suitors. Bucks will scent-check food sources while looking for these does, which makes a runway stand a good choice for bowhunters.

most mature does in the herd come into estrus. Because we're not talking about a lot of does, you're not going to see the widespread rut activity we expect in November. Rather, this activity is confined to the home area of the doe that comes into heat."

All this made perfect sense. Because there are only a few does in heat at this time, they attract a lot of bucks. I've yet to see a hot doe attract only one suitor during the mini-rut. This is very similar to what happens during the so-called second rut, which occurs about a month after the main rut. During this period a few does that did not conceive or were not bred during the November rut will cycle back into estrus. Also, in many areas, a percentage of fawns will enter their first estrus cycle about this same time, but because these numbers are nothing compared to the November rut, each doe or fawn in heat now attracts a number of bucks.

Why the action so often takes place in the same area year after year can probably be explained by food sources. The dominant doe lays claim to the best habitat and food sources in any given area. This is nature's way of ensuring the continuation of the species. Bucks, which in nature's scheme are dispensable, have to get by on less succulent forage. Even if an old doe dies, another doe—probably one of the old doe's mature daughters—will take over as the matriarchal doe and lay claim to the prime habitat. So around the best food sources you can figure there will be an old doe ruling the roost, and because it appears that only old does have an early estrus, these prime areas are the places to look for early rut action.

OCTOBER 12 TO 16: THE MAGIC DATES

In the Midwest, others and myself have witnessed this brief flurry of breeding activity from October 12 to 16. However, I'll admit that there have been seasons when I've hunted these days and not seen any rut activity. There are a couple of reasons why this doesn't surprise me. One is that you have to be in the right place at the right time. Remember that this activity is not taking place in every woodlot and on every ridge like it is during the November rut. The other reason is that this brief October fling is probably tied to the moon phases just like the main rut. After reading *Hunting Whitetails by the Moon* by Charles Alsheimer, I'm more convinced than ever that the moon plays a major role in determining the annual timing of breeding activity. This being the case, it makes sense that the October rut is on a similar schedule, which means that it is probably not happening every year between October 12 and 16. I'm going to be paying a lot more attention to moon phases in the next few years, and perhaps I'll be able to come up with a "schedule" that will allow me to predict the timing of the October mini-rut just as Alsheimer has done for the November rut.

HUNT THE FOOD SOURCES

From what I have seen and been able to glean from others, hunting food sources is the key to getting in on this mini-rut action. Scrapes and rubs appear to be after-the-fact evidence that something has gone on. By that I mean that the scrapes and rubs I've seen in conjunction with the October mini-rut have been made by bucks that are actually in the company of an estrus doe. Hunting over them is at best a long shot because it is unlikely that the buck that made them will return. What scrapes tell me at this time of year is that I've found an area where a buck—likely a mature buck—has interacted with an estrus doe. It is a spot I will remember for the following year.

The best advice I can offer on where to hunt during this period is to concentrate on areas where you routinely see does. Each doe family group is made up of a dominant doe, her offspring, and their offspring. If you know of a place where one or more of these family units feed, odds are good that one of those old gals will enter estrus during this mid-October window.

STILL A MYSTERY

I don't pretend to understand the full implications of the October rut. Why it occurs is anyone's guess. My theory is that by having the oldest does bred prior to the main rut, nature ensures that the dominant bucks will breed the best mothers. During the November rut, when a great number of does are in estrus at one time, it would

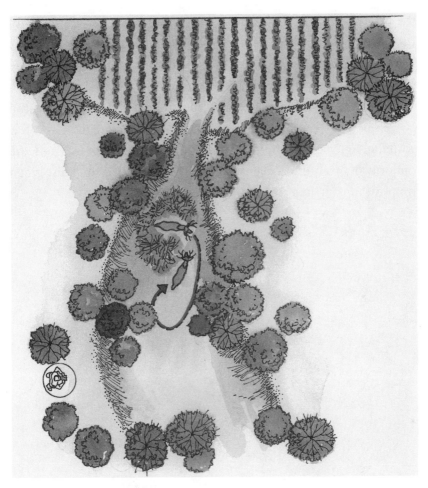

As food sources are the main drawing cards for does during the early rut, bucks will be consistently close by. Look for them in thick-cover staging areas near fields.

be possible for an old doe to enter estrus and either not be bred or be serviced by a lesser buck.

One other note is that all of my personal data (and most of what I've gleaned from others) has been from Midwestern states, namely Iowa, Minnesota, Wisconsin, Illinois, Missouri, Kansas, Michigan, Nebraska, and the Dakotas. I assume that the timing of the mini-rut would be similar in the Northeast, but what happens in the South I do not know. It might be that because the rut in many regions of the South is spread out over a longer period, pinpointing an October mini-rut would be very difficult.

The October mini-rut is not to be compared to the main rut in November, but there is no doubt in my mind that each fall a few whitetails engage in some serious breeding behavior without the majority of bowhunters ever realizing it. Hopefully, you'll discover a mini-rut in your area and capitalize on it.

2

HITTING THE RUT RIGHT

by Greg Miller

*Hunting the "search" and "breeding" phases of the rut
requires slightly different strategies.*

It was one of the most memorable morning hunts I've ever had. In just more than thirty minutes I watched five different bucks approach my decoy. The first buck, a good-looking 2½-year-old nine-pointer, approached in classic fashion. With his ears pinned back and hair standing on end, the young deer closed the final twenty yards in a stiff-legged, sideways-shuffling walk. The buck circled the decoy three times before catching on that something wasn't right. But even then he didn't spook. He threw one last menacing glare at the decoy and walked off toward the nearby woods.

The next three bucks were substantially larger. In fact, I judged each of them to be in the 140 class. They waltzed out to the picked cornfield where I was set up approximately five minutes apart. The first was a heavy-racked ten-pointer and seemed destined to take a ride in the back of my pickup, but what had initially appeared to be a done deal suddenly became a close-but-no-cigar situation. The ten-pointer got within forty yards, then abruptly turned and walked back the way he'd come. The next two bucks did the same thing — leaving me frustrated, to say the least.

It hurt bad enough to see those three bucks walk off, but the pain was nothing like what I experienced fifteen minutes later. That's when "Mr. Wonderful" arrived on the scene. This buck's massive ten-point rack was adorned with several sticker points. I judged his inside spread to be more than twenty inches, and there was no doubt in my mind that his gross score would exceed 180 points.

Initially, it appeared that the monster whitetail was going to end up right at the decoy. Indeed, he'd cut the distance between us to a mere thirty yards. But at that point he stopped and stared hard at the decoy. And the more he stared, the more suspicious he became. I must admit that I briefly considered taking a shot — but I just as quickly put it out of my head. The big deer was standing at an angle that gave me serious doubts about whether I could make a fatal shot.

The ten-pointer stared at the decoy for perhaps thirty seconds before making his move: turning and walking straight away from me. I quickly hung up my bow and grabbed my binoculars. One look through the glasses confirmed that I hadn't overestimated the size of his rack. He was every bit a 180-class animal. (Another hunter killed the buck a few days later, and his gross typical score was 183⅝.)

WHEN IS "PEAK" RUT?

Every one of the trophy deer hunters I know is obsessed with timing his hunt to coincide with the peak of the rut. Interestingly, some of these hunters are in total disagreement about what exactly constitutes peak rut. Some contend that the peak occurs when mature bucks aggressively start looking for receptive does (which is the search phase). Others argue that it takes place when the majority of mature bucks in an area are involved with breeding.

Think about it for a second. Which of these periods do you consider the rut's peak? I'd be surprised if there wasn't an equal split among hunters when it comes to answering this question. I personally consider the peak to be when the majority of mature bucks are paired up with does. This doesn't mean, however, that I consider this to be the best time to try to ambush a rutting whitetail.

Most hunters prefer to concentrate the bulk of their efforts on "peak rut" time. However, it would appear that there's some confusion as to what exactly constitutes peak rut.

There are some distinct differences between the strategies that are most effective during the rut's search phase and those that produce during the actual breeding phase. However, a good many hunters don't understand that they need to use different strategies during the two time frames. Both of the phases can be short-lived, especially when you consider that most hunters concentrate their efforts on relatively small areas. Unless you know which phase you're dealing with and what strategies are most effective during that phase, you could find yourself out of the game.

THE SEARCH PHASE

The hunt described earlier was one of my most memorable, even though I never drew my bow. Never before had so many big bucks been around me during a thirty-minute period. It was an incredible and unforgettable morning. I remember thinking at the time that the hunt was a perfect example of what can happen during the search phase of the rut.

In simplest terms, the search phase is when mature bucks are aggressively searching for receptive does. Luckily, a good deal of this activity takes place during daylight hours. Another thing that can work to our benefit is that mature bucks almost always start searching for receptive does within their home ranges.

This fact was responsible for my memorable morning. According to the fellow who owns the land where I had hunted, all four of the mature bucks I saw were resident deer. He'd seen every one eating in his fields numerous times throughout late summer and early fall. In fact, the four bucks actually were "bachelored up" and traveling together at the time.

The four certainly weren't bachelored up when I saw them later in the fall; however, they were still hanging around their core area. And it was obvious that they were aggressively searching for receptive does. This is exactly why I so love to hunt during the initial stages of the search phase. It's entirely possible that every mature buck in a particular core area could end up walking by my stand—perhaps within minutes of each other!

SEARCH-PHASE STRATEGIES

My favorite search-phase strategy entails setting up in spots I know big bucks will use when they're in search mode. In farmland terrain there are a couple such spots that always catch my eye. Brushlines that run between large chunks of cover are going to garner a lot of my attention. I'm also going to spend some time hunting near points of timber that jut out into open areas.

In most cases, mature bucks will stick fairly close to brushlines when traveling from one piece of cover to another. This just about ensures that they'll pass by within bow range of my stands. Therefore, I don't always incorporate a decoy into my brushline setups. I do, however, like to use rattling antlers and a grunt call. At this time of year I'm confident there's always at least one big buck wandering around within hearing range of my position. And at no other time during the season are mature bucks more likely to respond positively to calling.

Unlike with my setups along brushlines, I always use a decoy when I set up near timbered points. The reason is that dozens of past experiences have taught me that mature bucks don't always exit or enter timbered points at the same places. I've also learned that trying to relocate to the right spot is usually nothing more than an exercise in futility. It seems you're always one step behind.

By adding a decoy to my setups, I can actually *make* the right spot. Let's say a big buck pops out of the timber seventy-five yards from my stand. Without a decoy, I could pretty much write off the incident as just another no-shot encounter. With a decoy in the mix, I can almost bet that the buck will want to get a closer look. Actually, there's a good chance he'll walk right up to the decoy. At that point it should be game, set, and match.

Of course, big bucks frequent other spots besides brushlines and timbered points during the search phase. The most reliable way to find such spots is by simply observing when you're out at this time of year. Seeing a single big buck cruising through a particular spot might not appear to be much of a revelation, but I can assure you it is.

To begin with, it's a given that the same big buck will cruise through the spot again in the near future. Even more important, however, is the fact that any other big bucks that cruise through will take pretty much the same line as the buck you saw. I've seen countless examples of this. Oh, and by the way, mature bucks display a real propensity for using the same search-phase travel routes year after year. Find one of these hotspots, and you could be on your way to a string of successful seasons.

Mature bucks become active during the day just prior to the peak breeding period. This time is often referred to as the "search phase."

BREEDING-PHASE TACTICS

Any whitetail hunter worth his salt knows that mature bucks stick very close to does during the breeding phase. Primary feeding areas, doe/fawn bedding areas, and the runways that connect these two locales will play host to a good deal of big-buck activity. However, ambushing a big buck during the breeding phase usually involves a bit more than merely setting up near a feeding area, on the downwind side of a bedding area, or along a well-traveled runway.

The first thing hunters must realize is that not all deer food sources hold an equal amount of appeal. Though there may be a multitude of feeding opportunities available in a given area, the antlerless deer that live there will almost surely be concentrating their attentions on only one or two spots.

I take time prior to the breeding phase to find out exactly where the antlerless deer in my hunting areas prefer to feed. Actually, it doesn't take all that much time or effort to find these areas. In some cases I can accomplish this by driving through just before dark and glassing crops.

In those cases when the deer are feeding primarily in the woods, such as on acorns or browse, I'll simply do a bit of legwork during the midday hours. Trust me, it's not that difficult to figure out exactly where a bunch of deer are feeding in the woods. A couple of tip-offs are numerous and concentrated piles of droppings, as well as runways that are literally stomped down to the dirt.

Though I always strive to get my in-woods/feeding-area setups situated in the right spots, I sometimes discover during my first hunt that I'm slightly out of position. If this happens, I don't panic. Instead, I return to the area at midday and relocate my stand to a spot that will allow me to take advantage of my findings. It's my intent to get my stand positioned well within bow range of where I saw the most antlerless activity.

I almost always include a buck decoy in my setups when I hunt along the edges of cropfields. This is because of the unpredictable behavior displayed by rutting bucks. You can never really be sure which direction they'll come from when they approach a cropfield. Nor can you be sure of what they're going to do once they get there. Including a buck decoy can greatly increase your odds of having a big buck come within bow range. A big buck that is visiting a cropfield to check for estrus does is going to view the decoy as competition. And a big buck that follows a sequestered doe to the feeding area is going to view the decoy as a threat. In either case, it's almost a given that the buck is going to challenge this "trespasser."

One of my most memorable decoy hunts took place in Illinois several years ago. I was set up near the edge of a cut soybean field where I'd seen a lot of antlerless deer feeding the previous afternoon. Prior to climbing into my treestand, I placed a buck decoy in the beans approximately twenty yards straight out from my stand. An hour later a lone doe trotted out to the field some seventy-five yards from me. I could instantly tell by her behavior that she was "hot."

A few minutes later a big buck emerged from the timber and strolled out to join the doe. The buck immediately spotted my decoy. He laid back his ears and started toward it in an aggressive walk. I waited until the buck was a mere fifteen yards away before sending an arrow through his vitals.

There are other strategies that can be effective during the search and breeding phases, but I've had my greatest success using the methods outlined here. The secret behind making these strategies work lies in first recognizing which rut phase the bucks in your hunting areas are in. Then you must act quickly and accordingly.

3

SLOW STALKING THE RUT

by Bob McNally

Because most hunters are so treestand oriented, few of them
purposely stalk rutting whitetails. But it's a radical tactic that
just may produce that high-rack trophy of a lifetime.

I arrived late one October night for my annual Iowa whitetail bowhunt, so I had no time to scout the tangled draw where I normally place a treestand. I spoke to my friend Veryl Van Houtan, the farmer-landowner, and he said he'd seen several 140-plus bucks in "my" draw and thought I'd have no trouble locating a hot stand. But the place where he'd seen most of the bucks was 500 yards from the creek area where I usually climb a tree.

He described a prominent place in the draw to shinny up a tree with my Ol' Man climbing stand that next morning. But an hour before daybreak, traipsing around in the draw thickets, briers and oaks, I decided instead to sit down with my back next to an oak and wait for first light before choosing a spot to climb in the area of the draw he recommended.

Over the next thirty minutes it grew increasingly colder, and just before dawn it started to snow—hard. By the time I could see well enough to find a decent spot to climb a tree, there was an inch of white stuff on the ground.

With my stand on my back, my pack in one hand, bow and arrows in the other, I headed into the thicket between two large hardwood ridges. I hadn't walked 200 yards when movement caught my eye. Through the heavy-falling, sideways-blowing snow, a gigantic doe materialized. She wasn't running, just walking fast, tail up and jittery. She was only forty yards away and never looked at me, just kept moving along the edge of the thickest draw tangles, then cut back into the draw jungle 100 yards away.

Weird, I thought, that she didn't even spook from me.

Then, suddenly, the reason for her odd behavior appeared right on her tail—an enormous buck, every bit of 250 pounds, with ten tall, stark-white points and gross scoring easily 150 Pope & Young points. Trotting nose to the ground and oblivious to me, the buck took the same trail as the doe and disappeared.

The rut was obviously rocking, and I'd found what looked to be a hotspot, so I quickly walked to the trail the deer followed, checked the wind, and looked for a likely tree to climb. As I stood there with stand, pack, and bow, I heard something and looked up to see the doe coming back. She passed at fifteen yards, then ducked back into the draw thicket just as I saw the pursuing buck, seventy yards down the draw, following her every step and grunting like a hungry hog coming to corn.

As quickly as possible I dropped the pack, found my caliper re-lease, nocked an arrow, and, shaking, tried to get my composure as the buck came on, tracking the doe. At thirty-five yards, while using a tree as camouflage, I raised the bow, drew, and waited for the buck to step out at fifteen yards. But the buck had other ideas. Instead of following the doe, he cut her off in the thicket and never offered a shot. I stood there on the ground for twenty minutes, watching and waiting, but never saw that buck again—at least not that morning.

I climbed a tree and sat there until noon. The draw was full of deer, running upwind and downwind, crosswind, over the creek, and cutting up and down nearby ridges. I saw two other bucks that morning, including a dandy eight-point that easily would have made Pope & Young. He, too, was chasing a doe in the draw, as was a smaller six-point. I was confident about the place, and spent the whole week bowhunting the draw and passing many chances at bucks. At the time I thought I did the right thing. But never again will I sit tight in a tree when the bucks are going bonkers chasing does, especially when the weather is snowy, rainy, or windy. Instead, I'll put the wind in my face, get halfway up a ridge, and in full camouflage, still-hunt—just as I would with a firearm.

WHY WALK?

Still-hunting is radical whitetail archery thinking, especially for me, as I'm a dedicated treestand bowman. But it's finally sunk in that over the years some of the biggest bucks I've seen during the rut have been while I was walking to and from treestands. I spotted the two biggest whitetails I've ever seen this way, both in Illinois, both Boone & Crockett–class animals. It was during the rut, as bucks ran or tracked does along cornfield and hardwood edges, and I was walking to a stand or scouting. In both cases, I bowhunted those deer hard for a week from stands. I never saw either deer from a tree, and I've often wondered if I would have done better still-hunting for them.

When deer go bananas during the rut I'm convinced it's tough to take an outsize buck with standard bowhunting tactics, simply because bucks invariably do the unexpected. They are completely unpredictable, traveling day and night on trails and across open country they ordinarily wouldn't traverse. Further, during the hard rut, you can get surprisingly close to a mature buck whose brain is dizzy and eyes glassy from abundant doe estrus. Close enough, in fact, for a bow shot that's almost impossible to get at any other time.

Bowhunters who know how to still-hunt and use proven rattling and grunt call techniques to their advantage are almost assured of having more shot opportunities at good bucks than they would from a typical treestand spot.

Another plus for staying on the move with bow in hand during the rut is that you might discover a place that looks like a whitetail singles bar. Locate a small area with a dozen or more scrapes the size of Toyota truck hoods, with trails beat to the dirt and saplings the size of your forearm rubbed raw, and you'd be wise to hang a stand. But when the rut peaks, until you find such a spot, you're probably better off stalking, at least if a big buck is your target.

Don't believe it? Consider this: A few years ago I met Ernie Callandrelli from Quaker Boy Game Calls in Unionville, Missouri for five days of bowhunting out of the Unionville Sportsman's Club. First day out Callandrelli and I were in the thick of things with rutting whitetails. We each had lovesick deer in bow range, including several bucks, but we were holding out for big boys.

One morning I saw several deer and dozens of turkeys, but no bucks worth shooting. Late that morning I heard dogs barking, and two hounds came racing through the area chasing deer (including three bucks, one a dandy ten-point Pope & Young) and turkeys ahead of them. I hunted the same stand that afternoon, but didn't see a deer or turkey. The dogs, I figured, had pushed game around, and it would take a few hours for things to get back to normal. But the next morning I saw no deer, and didn't even hear a turkey.

All the good deer Bob McNally saw over the years while walking to and from treestands convinced him that stalking was a viable hunting option during the rut.

My confidence shattered, I pulled down my treestand to relocate to a hardwood ridge across a creek. With my stand on my back I clambered out of the woods, crossed the creek, and started into a head-high weedfield. Just into the field, and only eighty yards from my old treestand, I glanced upwind to my right and there stood a buck and doe. The buck was huge, but I didn't dare count points.

Then they turned and started walking slowly away. I nocked an arrow, figured the distance at twenty yards, grabbed my grunt call, and blew it once softly. The buck stopped and turned, then I drew, anchored, aimed and released.

The Beman shaft was there in a flash, the two-blade, 2¾-inch-wide Game Tracker Stiletto flying perfectly. Both deer immediately bolted through the field and disappeared in a second. I watched a greenfield on a hill in line with where they were headed, and in seconds saw the doe rocketing across the open—but not the buck. I walked to the spot where the deer stood and found my arrow and a good blood trail. I parted some grass for a better look at the trail, and I could see a bedded buck's rack. For long minutes I watched the deer, but it was dead, having traveled only thirty-one steps before falling.

The 4½-year-old deer weighed an estimated 280 pounds and sported double brow tines full of cedar shavings from rubbing bark with a rut-swollen neck. He had 15 "scoreable" points, 5½-inch main beam circumferences, and a 17-inch inside spread with 22-inch main beams. He easily made Pope & Young, grossing 161⅜ points.

Still skeptical about stalking bucks during the rut?

Ponder this story from West Virginia bowhunter Harold McCoy, a diehard still-hunter. In his home country, McCoy has learned from long experience that he sees more whitetails if he still-hunts into the wind, and he's taken lots of good deer this way with his bow.

On one occasion, it was November 7 and bucks were in rut, chasing does. McCoy was still-hunting on public land in rugged Boone County, not far from bow-only Logan County. He was after a very specific buck, one he'd seen the previous year, three different times over a sixteen-day rut period. McCoy believed the buck was crossing back and forth between Boone and Logan Counties, courting and chasing does. The rut is the only time McCoy believes a

West Virginia bowman walking rugged terrain can have a good chance at taking a mountain monster buck, so he was in the woods as much as possible. He also believed that a rifle hunter would likely collect "his" buck when the gun season opened if McCoy failed in his bowhunting quest.

All sightings of the buck were made within a half-mile area, and McCoy was beginning to pattern the deer. He believed the buck was checking scrapes at night along a woods road. So early one morning he was still-hunting near thick cover adjacent to the scrape line. Suddenly he saw the buck moving quickly on the heels of a doe. McCoy knew he had to shoot or risk spooking the deer. He drew his 76-pound PSE Buckmaster bow, placed his one sight pin high over the buck's back, and loosed an arrow. It struck the buck high and back a bit, but with perseverance and good tracking skills McCoy recovered the animal.

The eleven-point deer was the best taken by a West Virginia bowhunter in 1996, touting a score of 163⅝ points.

While some archers like McCoy believe their best chance to take a rutting trophy buck is by careful still-hunting during the peak of the rut, many bowmen who score on good bucks from the ground do it by accident, just as I did in Missouri during the hunt described earlier. This "accidental" success by bowmen happens so frequently throughout whitetail country, that more archers should reconsider how they hunt during the rut—from a treestand, or on the ground.

Consider the case of Maryland bowhunter Jeff Hinson, who now lives in northern Florida. Hinson was in the Navy, stationed at the Patuxent Naval Test Center, and he'd heard about an enormous buck that had been seen by several friends and hunters on the base. Jeff, like a number of other hunters, became obsessed with taking the huge buck. He scouted religiously, often driving roads at night with his family. Finally he spotted the massive buck briefly one night, but never saw the buck during the day that year.

Bowhunters who seriously still-hunt often locate scrape lines and noteworthy rubs, which help them zero in on whitetail hotspots.

No one bagged the buck that year, and Hinson was convinced the deer survived the season. When the bow season opened the following fall, Hinson hunted only the giant whitetail, passing many smaller bucks and scouting intently for rubs and scrapes made by the monarch. He found sign he believed the huge buck had made and placed treestands in the area, which he hunted carefully and religiously, but to no avail. He saw many other bucks from his stands, but never the great whitetail.

Finally, late one morning, Hinson was walking down a trail toward a stand, and there, at twenty yards, stood the massive buck—neck swollen, eyes glazed from the rut. Hinson quickly drew his bow, aimed, and released his arrow. The shaft flew true, and the deer ran but a short distance before collapsing. It weighed 235 pounds, had six points on one side, seven points on the other with a twenty-inch inside spread. It scored 152 typical points, easily qualifying for Pope & Young.

If you still believe bowhunters who stalk must be lucky instead of good to take a buster buck, think about this story from Kentucky archer Greg Powers. He knew some good bucks lived on the Paintsville Lake Wildlife Management Area in northeast Kentucky, so he walked over a mile back into a remote spot of the 12,000-acre public hunting area. He had no treestand and was just slowly still-hunting along a white-oak ridge looking for rutting buck sign when he heard a deer approaching from just below the ridge crest.

"The buck came from the bottom of the hill, through a huge thicket of honeysuckle vines," Powers recalls. "He was making a lot of noise, and when I first saw him all I could see was honeysuckle tangled in his rack. As soon as the buck got on top of the ridge he started rubbing a tree eight inches in diameter. I was gawking at the rack so long my arrow fell off the bow rest. Then the buck stepped behind a tree.

"He was just twenty yards away. The sun was at my back, wind in my favor, and he was in full rut—neck swollen huge. He stepped out from behind the tree, I drew and let my arrow fly."

Spine shot, the buck dropped instantly. With help from two friends Powers dragged the buck down to a lake, where they got the deer out by boat. The 5½-year-old whitetail had an estimated live weight of 230 pounds, with 21 non-typical points and a 20-inch inside antler spread. The rack officially scored 200 non-typical inches, easily qualifying for the Pope & Young and Boone & Crockett record books.

So next time bucks are rutting hard, and you're not seeing deer like you should, think about slow stalking. Keep the wind in your favor, and employ calling, rattling, scent cover, camouflage, and stealthy skills to your best advantage. And use those optics, both quality binoculars to scan terrain well ahead and rangefinders to pinpoint your target, which is usually moving during the rut.

Doing something radical sometimes can make a big difference in bowhunting success. Besides, if you're not getting opportunities at heavy-beam bucks on stand, what have you got to lose by stretching your legs?

4

FORGET ABOUT HUNTING SCRAPES

by John Weiss

*New evidence reveals that hunting scrapes is not as
effective as hunters once thought. However, knowing
where scrapes are can be critical to rut-hunting success.*

Let's be perfectly honest. Over the years you've digested all the hype about hunting scrapes. You've learned where they're most frequently found and how to distinguish between different sizes and types of scrapes. Moreover, you've invested a ton of time sitting on stands overlooking scrapes. And I'll bet you've had very little success shooting big bucks over those scrapes.

It's important to note that your favorite hunting experts have not been intentionally misleading you. They've been hunting the same scrapes they've been recommending to others. But the world of whitetails holds many mysteries, and until we can teach the critters to talk we'll have to continue to second-guess what a lot of their woodland sign actually means to them and to other deer sharing that same habitat.

Fortunately, deer biologists are continually engaged in fieldwork: testing theories, tracking deer outfitted with radio-transmitter collars, using special cameras to record after-dark deer activity, and attempting to unravel still-unknown secrets of the love lives of whitetails. As a result, those who specialize in writing books and magazine articles about deer behavior are continually revising and updating both their work and the most effective hunting strategies currently known.

WHAT WE KNOW

Few things in the deer hunter's world trigger adrenaline-pumping excitement like finding a fresh scrape with large tracks in it and then detecting the unmistakable, pungent aroma of tarsal scent wafting about the area. So it wasn't at all surprising one day when I chanced upon a mother lode of scrapes and my pacemaker almost short-circuited. In an area no larger than about two acres I counted twenty-seven of the mating invitations, indicating a mature buck that had literally gone loco with breeding frenzy.

This electrifying discovery brought still another revelation. For the first time in a long career of pursuing whitetails, I no longer pondered whether the mating signs before my eyes were primary scrapes, secondary scrapes, boundary scrapes, or whatever. It just didn't make any difference what label a human might attach to them. In terms of whitetail communication, they all stood for the same thing—a very special place where a buck intended to pass on his gene pool. Moreover, it was a place that literally screamed "Hunt here!"

Within an hour I'd hung a portable stand in a strategic location within shooting range of six of the scrapes. During the next seven days I saw a ten-pointer in the general area just once and he showed little

Rather than using scrape lines as ambush areas, study where bucks are headed to and coming from. What you need to find are doe bedding areas. These are the best places to take a rutting buck.

interest in actually approaching any of the scrapes. The closest he came to one of them was sixty yards, far beyond my bowhunting skill.

A few things we are pretty confident about concerning buck scraping behavior is that scrapes are some sort of catalyst that serve to unite bucks and does during the rut. Since we are sure that various types of scents are deposited in and around scrape areas, we suspect that scrapes also transmit various forms of information to other deer when the author of a given scrape is not in the immediate area.

We also know that the manner in which a buck makes scrapes is far from a random occurrence. We've filmed the manner in which bucks paw out their scrapes, rub-urinate in them, and mutilate the overhead tree branch that virtually always is a hallmark of each scrape's location.

Moreover, in conducting radio-telemetry studies, with deer wearing collars outfitted with transmitters, we've discovered that in a majority of cases each buck's many scrapes are systematically strung out in linear fashion, with the actual length of each scrape line being determined by the population density of animals in the immediate area. Understandably, in regions where deer numbers are relatively low, bucks must travel farther during the rut to encounter receptive females; as a result, the scrape lines made by these bucks may cross many miles of terrain. Conversely, where deer numbers are high and bucks don't have to aggressively search and advertise for does, scrape lines are far shorter in length.

Aside from the differences in scrape-line length, biologists also have learned something that both long and compacted scrape lines have in common. In plotting the movements of radio-collared deer on maps, we've discovered that most scrape lines resemble a "star" or "cross" pattern. In other words, a given buck puts down two scrape lines, one running north-and-south, the other strung out on east-and-west. Even more interesting, the two lines usually intersect approximately at their midpoints.

Currently, we don't know exactly why this phenomenon occurs, so this is where we have to become theoretical. One educated guess (don't hang your hat on this, because we may entirely change our thinking next year) is that one of the scrape lines is designated for daytime use and the other is reserved for night activity. Even more likely, however, is that by laying down scrapes so they are linear in direction and in line with compass points, a buck engineers many different travel options for checking his scrapes in accordance with a given day's wind direction.

PUTTING THEORY INTO ACTION

Several years ago I attempted to use this insight to pattern bucks in my favorite hunting area. It seemed logical to assume that if I intensely scouted the terrain, found all the scrapes in existence, and then plotted their exact locations on a topo map, I could ascertain scrape lines forming the star configuration. Then I could easily peg the intersection of the lines and hunt there. Taking a nice buck would amount to child's play.

As it often happens, however, even the best of plans sometimes fizzle. With other bucks sharing the same range and laying down their own scrape lines, I quickly realized the futility of attempting to identify the specific scrape lines made by one buck. It was then that researchers at the University of Georgia came to my rescue with a new insight.

Although they couldn't explain exactly why, there's a strong suggestion from a buck's scrape-revisitation activity that not all of his scrapes are of equal value to him. So apparently it's not all that worthwhile to try to dope out the star or cross configurations of scrape lines. Just keep in mind that at intermittent locations along the length of his two scrape lines, a mature buck establishes several core rutting areas that occupy most of his attention.

Along the length of the north/south axis of a scrape line, for example, there may be a lone, insignificant scrape every 100 yards for a distance of a half-mile. Then suddenly, for no apparent reason, there may be ten or twenty scrapes clustered in an area the size of a football field. Several similar situations may exist along the east/west scrape line. If a hunter can key in upon one of these major rutting areas, there's a much higher probability he'll fill his tag.

But don't begin doing cartwheels just yet. Clemson University in South Carolina recently released the results of a study by deer biologist Karen Dasher, who has been a pioneer in the use of remote-sensing cameras to monitor deer behavior at scrapes. Her study finding, which many of us have long suspected, was that a whopping eighty-five percent of all scrape visits by bucks occur after dark.

So consider this: Even if a hunter has somehow managed to find a buck's number-one primary scrape, which in itself is an incredible odds-defying accomplishment, on a given day he'll have to sit at that scrape from dawn until dusk (about twelve hours) just to have only a fifteen percent chance of seeing the buck!

Personally, I've got better things to do with my time. Like first accepting Karen Dasher's insight that the immediate areas around scrapes are not productive places to hunt. Then, in forsaking scrape hunting, to concentrate upon her further advice to instead hunt trails from bedding sites to and from scraping areas.

In going back to the beginning of this report, the hot concentration of scrapes I found was a rather common occurrence in that area. It's not necessary for me to describe the exact location of this find, though, because these rutting areas have well-defined characteristics that seem to hold true throughout whitetail country. The only must-have tool for finding these hotspots is a topo map or aerial photo of your hunting area.

Keep in mind when studying your map or photo that whitetail bucks very rarely make scrapes on steep-sloping terrain. Try to recall the scrapes you've found in the past and I'll bet a month's rent the vast majority of them, even those in mountain areas, were found on predominantly level ground. The flat terrain may have consisted of nothing more than a terraced hillside bench winding around a mountainside, but it probably was relatively level.

Bill Williamson, a long-time hunting partner of mine who is an expert in locating major rutting areas, advises hunters to also eliminate the edges of large croplands, fields, and meadows.

"Finding scrapes dotting the perimeters of such landforms is quite common," Bill explains. "But these scrapes will lie to you. They're visited almost exclusively after full dark and they're not where the buck in question engages in intense rutting activity."

Whitetails generally put down scrape lines in areas that offer a mix of mature and immature trees and successive understory brush and vegetation. They tend to scrape infrequently in large, endless tracts of mature forestland.

This field of beans might look like nirvana, but hunting the numerous scrapes along its edge will not likely pay off. They are visited almost exclusively after dark.

An astute hunter can therefore systematically eliminate from consideration three areas: Those with any appreciable slope, those where mature high-canopy forests predominate, and the perimeters of crops and fields. This elimination process should then allow him to relatively easily identify on his map or aerial photo those areas worth an on-the-spot investigation.

Last year, Williamson and I were hunting gently rolling farmlands in central New York when we found a textbook-perfect illustration of a major rutting area. Ten years earlier, our landowner host had logged 100 acres of mature timber, but he had harvested only the choice walnut and oak trees and all others were left standing.

Well, the absence of a shade-producing high canopy during that ten-year period had allowed a profusion of saplings and woody plant life to spring up, creating the diverse habitat that cover-loving whitetails favor. In addition, despite gentle undulations in the terrain here and there, the topography of this particular segment of real estate was basically flat.

A casual observer might have next interpreted our rather brief hike through the area as a sloppy, half-hearted scouting endeavor, but we knew precisely what we were doing. We had already studied a map and eliminated the perimeters of the farmer's two pastures and cornfield and alfalfa meadows. We also discounted a steep ridgeline of white oaks (acorn bearing oaks, no less!) the landowner had not yet harvested. At other times of year, these food sources would have been worth a look. But we were intent on scrape hunting, and because the region's does were approaching the start of their estrus cycles, we were certain the local bucks would be devoting their energies to mating rather than to feeding. Moreover, the former logging area was the only place on the farmer's several hundred acres where all of the necessary components of a buck's preferred rutting area existed.

Bill and I began searching for scrapes and duly plotting each on our map. As the morning wore on, we finally pieced together what appeared to be at least one leg of a cross configuration running north/south. However, we were not able to identify the east/west scrape line, so we were left with only one course of action.

"I'll follow this scrape line heading north until it peters out," my partner suggested, "and you work it to the south. We'll meet back at the truck in two hours."

As it happened, Bill was the one to make an exciting discovery and when we later reunited he explained: "I was hiking north beyond the last scrape marked on our map. Scrape lines are never perfectly straight, so I was zigzagging slightly to cover a fifty-yard wide swath of ground, and I was finding a random scrape every seventy-five yards or so. Suddenly the breeze shifted a bit and I detected a strong urine-like aroma in the air. I headed toward the source, and moments later stepped into a clearing where the odor was so raunchy it was like being in a bus station bathroom."

The clearing, which was only one acre in size and surrounded by cover so thick it would have strangled a gopher, revealed one scrape after another peppering the ground. Bill counted nine of them and then beat a hasty retreat so that he wouldn't further disturb the area. He then wolfed down his lunch and quickly hustled back to the rutting area with a portable stand. He sat there the remainder of that day, and all day long for the next three days, and never saw a deer.

SORTING THROUGH THE CONFUSION

Even though it's quite possible to follow a scrape line as my partner did and eventually discover a large concentration of scrapes, exasperation is a never-ending part of the game. As mentioned earlier, trying to sort out which scrapes are part of a pattern can be confusing, at best. That's why it's so important, before you go afield, to use a map or aerial photo to identify areas where bucks are most likely to concentrate their scrapes. But then, rather than impulsively hunt the scraping area itself, the expert consensus is to study one's map or photo to first find the nearest heavy-cover area where the buck is likely bedding. Next, attempt to dope out the nighttime trail the deer is likely taking to the scrape area and place a stand overlooking that trail as close as possible to the bedding area.

Keep in mind that for much of the year, adult bucks and does live in different areas of their shared home ranges and seldom mingle with each other, but as the rut approaches they become inseparable. As a result, keeping tabs on the whereabouts of does can also play a key role in locating a buck's major rutting area.

On countless occasions I've bird-dogged a scrape line for a half-mile, eventually discovered a major rutting area and then, upon closer investigation, found a doe bedding area nearby. So now when I'm having a tough time following a scrape line or finding a rut area, I try to recall where I have found doe beds in the past. Once I've found such a doe bedding area, it's then relatively easy to study the surrounding several hundred yards of terrain where bucks are likely to have established their prime breeding grounds.

It's not difficult, even in unfamiliar terrain, to find doe bedding areas. Does prefer to bed in thickets midway up a slope or at the heads of drainages and hollows instead of in bottomlands or along ridge crests. The beds themselves are easily identified by the matted ovals of varying sizes that are indented in the grass and leaf litter and by large and small tracks leading in and out of the area; the smaller tracks and beds are those of the doe's current offspring and her daughter from the previous year.

It's also crucial to remember that mature bucks seem to favor the same major rutting areas year after year and will even lay down scrapes in the exact same spots they did the previous season. Telltale evidence of this can be seen by closely examining scrapes to see if they have a saucer-like appearance from repeated annual use. You're also likely to find fresh rubs on nearby saplings, along with healed scars from past years.

No one knows what bombshell research findings the deer biologists will next drop on us. But for the present time, forget hunting scrapes. Your hours on stand will be more greatly rewarded by instead finding buck bedding areas and then stand-hunting the trails those bucks will be using to visit their scrapes when night falls.

5

DO YOU SAVVY RUT SPEAK?

by John Weiss

Before you can walk the walk, you have to be able to talk the talk.

D eer biologists and hunting writers have their own scientific jargon to describe virtually every aspect of the whitetail's mating season. To benefit from the latest research, hunters must be on the same page. The following is a compendium of the most common "rut-speak" terms hunters should be familiar with to fully understand—and capitalize on—what researchers have to say about deer behavior.

Alpha buck—Also called the dominant buck. The buck in a local deer population that is not necessarily the oldest and does not necessarily have the largest antlers, but currently holds the highest social ranking.

Antler rub—A place on a sapling where a buck has removed the bark with his antlers. This is done not to remove velvet, as was previously believed, but to serve as a "signpost marker" that communicates the maker's presence and social standing to other bucks. As a rule, the larger the diameter of the tree rubbed, the bigger the buck.

Bachelor bucks—Small groups of males of the same approximate age and social ranking that live and travel together during spring, summer, and early fall, at which time they refine their social ranking by sparring. Shortly thereafter the bachelor

An alpha buck holds the highest social rank in a local deer population, although he may not always have the largest antlers.

group disbands and individual bucks begin adhering to their own areas in preparation for the breeding period.

Beta buck—Also called a subordinate buck. Males in the local deer population that usually (but not always) are young, immature, and of low social ranking.

Boundary scrapes—Scrapes that are created around the periphery of a buck's home range, often near natural barriers that the buck is not likely to cross, such as wide river courses, lakeshores, steep canyon walls, or vast open prairies.

Centrist rut—Rutting dates and breeding activity that fall within the norm, as compared to breeding activity in some years that occurs somewhat earlier or later than the norm (believed to be a result of different moon phases).

Chase phase—An approximate week-long component of the pre-rut period when bucks are anxious to breed and are in nonstop hot pursuit of does that are almost, but not quite, ready to accommodate them.

Community scrapes—Scrapes shared by several bucks that are usually the same age and hold relatively equal positions in the social hierarchy of the local deer herd.

Crepuscular-polyphasic—The level of deer activity in relation to light levels. "Nocturnal" creatures are those that operate exclusively at night, such as bats. "Diurnal" creatures are those that are strictly daylight-oriented, such as gamebirds. Deer lead crepuscular-polyphasic lifestyles, meaning that they may be up and around and engaging in various activities at any time of day or night, but that they prefer the lower-light levels of dawn and dusk.

Estrogen—The female sex hormone.

Estrus—Also referred to as "heat." The brief period in which a doe's endocrine system makes her receptive to being bred and makes her capable of conceiving.

Estrus-response scrape—A small, insignificant scrape made by a buck when he detects a doe's estrus urine on the ground. Not made in conjunction with an overhead branch, not revisited, and often found on doe trails and in open meadows where does have been feeding.

Fighting highly—Aggressive antler meshing during the breeding period, usually when one alpha (dominant) buck encroaches into the breeding area of another.

Flehmen response—Also known as "lip-curling." Named after the biologist who first identified and explained the behavior in which a buck tilts his head back, curls back his upper lip, and then inhales odors that are subsequently analyzed by the vomeronasal organ.

Forehead gland scent—A pheromone secreted by the hundreds of sebaceous glands just beneath the scalp on the forehead. Deposited on antler-rubbed saplings and licking branches to communicate to other deer the maker's sex and social status.

Gestation period—The length of time from when a doe conceives till she gives birth. For whitetails, the gestation period is 200 days.

Hypothalamus gland—A gland in the brain that releases various hormones involved in ovulation in does and sperm production in bucks. Also involved in the development of secondary sex characteristics such as antlers.

Interdigital gland scent—A waxy secretion from the interdigital gland, located between the deer's hoofs. Continually deposited as the deer walks, it communicates information to other deer, such as sex and age.

Licking branch—A low branch hanging over a scrape that a buck hooks with his antlers, chews, and deposits saliva and forehead gland scent on, especially during the pre-breeding period. Also, any low-hanging branch not in association with a scrape that bucks and does alike use as communication signposts throughout the year.

Metatarsal gland scent—From the metatarsal glands, located on the outside of the lower rear legs. An alarm pheromone to warn other nearby deer of impending danger.

Omega buck—A middle-aged buck that, in the presence of other bucks, may display either dominant or subordinate behavior in accordance with the ages and social status of other males.

Peak rut—An approximately two-week period of intense mating activity.

Photoperiodism—The diminishing ratio of daylight to dark, beginning with the autumnal equinox, that commands a deer's endocrine system to begin changing the animal's body chemistry in preparation for breeding.

Pineal gland—Also called the "vestigial third eye." A gland in the brain that, within two minutes of accuracy, measures the amount of light coming through a deer's eye and at a prescribed time triggers the onset of the rut.

Pituitary gland—A gland in the brain that receives electrical signals from the pineal gland and translates them into chemical signals, which are sent to the endocrine system, commanding it to flood the body system with sex hormones.

In many areas of the Midwest, a buck like this would likely be an omega buck despite its large rack.

Post-rut—An approximate four-week period in which bucks are recuperating from the rutting frenzy. It begins with intermittent "trolling" at the end of the peak rut, but quickly evolves into prolonged periods of bedding.

Posturing—Behavior exhibited by bucks and does alike when in the presence of other deer as a means of visually reinforcing their social ranking. This may include dominant displays, such as intent staring, holding the head high or raising the hair on the back of the neck. Or it may include subordinate displays, such as avoiding eye contact, holding the head low, holding the spine in a swayback manner or clamping the tail between the legs. In the case of dominant does, it also may involve standing on the back legs and kick-boxing. Posturing may be engaged in at any time of year, but it escalates just prior to the breeding season.

Preorbital gland scent—Once believed to be a communicative scent secreted by glands at the corners of the eyes, it's now considered a vestigial gland that may have served a purpose thousands of years ago but no longer does (and the accumulated matter in the corners of the eyes is nothing more than dried tear residue). When a buck is seen rubbing his eye area on licking branches, it's now believed that the nearby forehead glands are being used.

Preputial glands—Numerous, tiny glands found within a buck's penal sheath. No research-documented function, but believed by many biologists to play a role in breeding.

Pre-rut—An approximately two- to four-week period prior to the onset of actual breeding activity when bucks are staking out intended breeding areas, signposting with rubs and scrapes, finalizing their social ranking with other bucks, posturing in the presence of other males, and prowling for does that may be showing signs of entering estrus early.

Primary scrape—A particular scrape that a buck revisits on a far-more-frequent basis. Once believed to be the catalyst that brings a buck and a doe together; now believed to serve the stronger purpose of communicating a buck's social status to other bucks.

Priming pheromone—A secretion from the forehead glands that a buck deposits on antler-rubbed saplings. It is believed to proclaim his presence and social status among other bucks, to induce does into an earlier-than-usual estrus, and to psychologically repress younger bucks from breeding in that specific area. Airborne gland secretions, such as those from the metatarsal gland, are referred to simply as "pheromones."

Progesterone—A female hormone that aids in conception, maintains pregnancy, and promotes development of the mammary glands for the production of milk.

Rub line—A line of consecutive, relatively close antler-rubbed trees, usually created along a trail or through a travel corridor.

Rub-urinating—A procedure in which a deer squeezes its back legs together, hunches up its back and urinates so that the urine runs down the inside of the hind legs and over the tarsal glands to transfer tarsal scent to the ground.

Second rut—A replay of the first rut that takes place after the culmination of the primary breeding period. It is almost always of mild intensity and in some regions even nonexistent. It takes place mostly in regions where the sex ratios are greatly out of balance, with far more does than the available bucks can service. Those does that are not bred and those does that are bred but do not conceive lose heat after twenty-four hours and then experience a brief recurring estrus cycle twenty-eight days later. There are many known regions of the country where sex-ratio imbalances are so great (more than 30:1) that a third rut even takes place twenty-eight days after the second rut.

Secondary scrape—All scrapes begin life early in the season as secondaries. However, in time, certain ones become elevated in status to primary scrapes.

Social hierarchy—Also sometimes referred to as hierarchical ranking, social ranking, dominance scale, totem pole, or pecking order. The defined level of social status at which bucks and does find themselves in a local deer population; usually determined by a combination of sparring, posturing, bluffing, and each animal's age and state of health.

Sparring—Not to be confused with fighting, this is non-aggressive antler meshing prior to the breeding period by bucks attempting to establish or reinforce their social ranking.

Staging area—A place where bucks and does linger for an indeterminate length of time prior to engaging in an altogether different type of behavior, as when deer hold just inside the leading edge of cover waiting for dark before venturing into an open area to feed.

Tarsal gland scent—A musky pheromone from the tarsal glands, located on the inside of the rear legs at the hocks. When deposited on the ground through the process of rub-urinating, it identifies the sex and age of the animal to others.

Tending bond—When a buck remains very near a doe that is close to estrus and will not leave her side because the pheromones she's emitting are signaling that she's almost ready to breed.

Temporal rubs—Antler rubs made quickly and on a whim, often when bucks are posturing, and that do not involve aggressive removal of tree bark. Usually not found on trails or in conjunction with other nearby rubs and believed to have little significance compared to intentional signpost rubs.

Testosterone—The male sex hormone.

Trickle rut—A sharp reduction in daylight rutting intensity during a given year. Believed to be the result of abnormal weather phenomena, such as unseasonably hot weather that causes most breeding activity to take place after dark.

Trolling—Late breeding-period behavior on the part of bucks in which they travel widely in search of does that have not yet been bred, does that have been bred but did not conceive, or does that are destined to experience a slightly later-than-usual estrus.

Velvet—The soft, blood-rich "skin" that covers and nourishes a buck's antlers during their growing period. When antler growth is complete, the velvet quickly dries, cracks, and falls away in shreds. The process usually is completed within twenty-four hours and requires no rubbing on the part of the buck. Underneath, the antler beams and tines already are smooth, and the antler tips are pointed.

Vomeronasal organ—A diamond-shaped organ in the roof of the mouth that chemically analyzes odors, then converts that information into electrical stimuli and transmits it to the brain to elicit a behavioral response. Used mostly during the breeding season when bucks and does are emitting pheromones that communicate their stage of sexual readiness.

6

THE SEVEN PHASES OF THE RUT

by Curt Wells

Call me crazy, but here's my theory
on the rut—and how I hunt each part of it.

Two of the things I enjoy most about bowhunting whitetails are
the intimate nature of the hunt and the speculation, theory,
and conjecture that go with trying to decipher the hieroglyphics of
whitetail behavior.

No other type of hunting allows you to observe and study your
target animal—or any animal, for that matter—like bowhunting
does. You spend hours, days, and weeks in a tree or ground blind
watching and learning. The game is typically in a natural, unalarmed

state, and you see things you would never see during firearms season. And because bowhunting seasons are generally long, you can observe deer throughout an entire fall and early winter.

As we observe these magnificent and complex mammals, we develop our own theories and philosophies about their behavior. From our experiences, we conclude certain things and incorporate this information with the theories and ideas of other whitetail hunters, biologists, and experts. The results form our own personal whitetail philosophies, which govern the way we hunt. Because no one can think like a whitetail or know what a whitetail is thinking, the fun part is that most of what we know is based not on fact, but on theory and conjecture, which means that no one can say with impunity that our theories are categorically wrong.

On that note, the following is my own theory about the whitetail rut and how it relates to my hunting activity. I call it the "seven phases of the rut." You might think I'm a wacko. And you might be right. Then again . . .

PECKING-ORDER PHASE

Once while taking a two-day break from elk hunting, I spent some time bowhunting along the Musselshell River in Montana. Those were the days when there were countless deer—both muleys and whitetails—using the riverbottom. It was easy to get in some quality time watching deer behavior.

One particular incident involved a group of young whitetail bucks cavorting in the late-afternoon sun. They ranged from a forky to a 3 × 2, 3 × 3, 3 × 4, 4 × 4, and the monster of the group, a 4 × 5 with antlers about the size of your hands with your wrists tied together. All were 1½-year-old bucks with similar body sizes. The peculiar thing was that the buck with the most points invariably won the half-kidding sparring matches that occurred when they weren't munching succulent alfalfa. It became apparent that the 4 × 5 was the dominant buck, and that he knew it.

I've always wondered about that day. How did those bucks know whose antlers were biggest? Does it have something to do with testosterone levels? How does a buck know how big his own antlers are? From rubbing trees? Looking at himself in the water? I know this last question sounds ridiculous, but how do they know? And does it matter, or is something else the key?

The point is that the rut really begins with the establishment of the pecking order. Bucks hang together all summer long, then around late August things change. Soon their antlers harden and they start to push each other around. It's playful at first, but then nature takes the fun out of it. The pushing gets more forceful, and there are winners and losers. Once dominance is established, the fights become less frequent because a dominant buck can just give a head-fake, and a subordinate buck will back away.

Now I don't pretend to know the exact reason deer rub trees. I don't believe it has anything to do with removing velvet, and I seriously doubt it has anything to do with leaving trails to follow or any of that. I think rubbing is simply an act of frustration. Either a buck has no one to take his frustrations out on, or he prefers an opponent who won't fight back. I suppose rubs act as some sort of signposts, too—but of what, who knows? Regardless, this is the time when rubs appear, and that usually indicates the beginning of the next phase: the "separation phase."

Strategy: If I choose to hunt the first phase, it's probably because I've spotted a good buck with his bachelor group and decided he's worth fighting the mosquitoes and summer heat. I do my best to pattern the group's movement and get in the way. It's tough hunting, but not impossible.

SEPARATION PHASE

It doesn't take too many confrontations before bucks decide it's no longer a good time hanging out with the boys. The bucks have changed from buddies to competitors. Besides, they start to get these urges (which to the young bucks are inexplicable), and they have this overwhelming desire to sniff the south ends of northbound does. In other words, scent-check.

As September wanes, bucks have abandoned their bachelor groups and dispersed. The young bucks may begin to think about does. The bucks that have survived a handful of breeding seasons become more reclusive. That "big dog" you spotted with a group of smaller bucks in a beanfield in August has now become nocturnal.

In fact, most deer seem to virtually disappear at this time of year, making the separation phase a difficult time to hunt. It seems there is a significant dead period from late September through early October when deer movement is at a minimum. This isn't just my observation. I've talked to countless other bowhunters in different parts of the country who have experienced the same thing. There are exceptions, as always, but to me this lull is puzzling.

Strategy: I just go waterfowl hunting and leave the deer to their mysterious inactivity. I've spent too many fruitless hours in tree-stands at this time of year. Besides, I've usually just returned from a grueling elk hunt and need the rest.

SCRAPE PHASE

There are actually two scrape phases. The first is a false alarm, but worth noting. It occurs back in September, somewhere between the first two phases. In the fall, does come into estrus monthly, similar to humans. If not bred in November, they come back into estrus in December for the so-called second rut.

It seems logical to me that does also experience an estrus period, albeit a weak one, in September and October. This would account for the very early scraping activity that occurs around mid-September in my area. The associated scents, faint as they may be, trigger the reproductive instincts in young bucks that don't know better. For reasons they probably don't understand, they make scrapes.

That brings us back to October, when the genuine scraping activity occurs. I believe scrapes evolved to ensure procreation, particularly in times of low deer populations. Bucks lay down a scrape line far and wide, sort of like a dragnet. Does get wind of the calling card, show up for the party and bingo! — fawns on the way. It ensures that the two genders find each other.

Today, with excellent deer populations everywhere, scrapes are more of an instinctive rather than practical method for matching bucks with does. Once a doe comes into estrus these days, she doesn't have to go looking for a buck because there's been at least one glued to her rear end for three days. But the instinct is still there, and the scrapes show up, year after year, often in the same places, under the same overhanging branches. Instinct still drives a buck to check his scrapes and the scrapes of others, which means these calling cards will always have value to hunters.

Strategy: Good things can happen when you hang around scrapes, especially large "annuals," but I don't expect to see large bucks yet. I'm careful about spending too much time in my best rutting woods, opting to leave those areas alone until prime time. During this phase, rattling and grunting work well and seldom have a negative effect.

PRETENDER PHASE

This is when hunting gets exciting. It's the end of October now, and the inexperienced bucks are getting agitated. They have a very

Great things can happen when you hang around scrapes. You should look for them in the same general areas season after season.

good idea what they're supposed to do, but they just aren't getting any cooperation from the ladies. They even try the fawns, which run, too. Frustration builds, and some serious chasing begins. This can create chaos in your favorite deer woods, and if you're looking for just any buck, this is your best time to hunt.

The "pretenders," as I call them, don't give up easily because they can't understand what they're doing wrong. They don't know it's too early. It's comical to watch a young 3 X 3 running after a doe with a perplexed "why-is-she-running-away" look on his face.

The pretender phase is in full force when you see the fawns by themselves. They have been run off by the pretenders and won't likely get back with their mothers until the "breeding phase" is complete.

Strategy: Here's where the action begins to heat up. I love to use a decoy at this time of year and set it up as a buck. Use antlers just a bit smaller than the buck you hope to kill. A good buck isn't going to feel threatened by a little 4 X 4, so use antlers that threaten. I also do some grunting and bleating at this time, just to stir things up a bit. It's still not time for the big dogs, but adolescent bucks are going crazy and can provide opportunities.

BREEDING PHASE

For the trophy hunter, this is prime time. While the pretenders have been running themselves ragged, the big boys have been laying back in the thick brush shaking their heads in disgust. They've seen a few breeding seasons and learned there is no action to be had until the right scent rides the breeze. The nose knows.

When the time comes, the dominant bucks cautiously slip from their deepest, darkest sanctuaries and begin taking care of business. They easily reassert their dominance with as little as a head fake toward a subordinate buck. The big bucks take over the chase, picking the does that are ready to submit. The difference is that a big buck seldom has to chase them far. Instead, a dominant buck will

When the rut hits, anything can happen at any time. It pays to have all of your gear at the ready while in your treestand.

herd a doe into his lair, keeping her there like a cutting horse works a steer. He'll concentrate on that single doe until he breeds her; then he'll move on.

This is the time when a dominant buck can be vulnerable. He'll move more during daylight hours because his doe is moving then. He may be a veteran, but he's not thinking as clearly as he does the rest of the year. His mission is focused, and he is not easily distracted by things that would otherwise send him into flight. The survival instinct becomes weaker than the instinct to procreate.

Strategy: This is the time when I like to switch my buck decoy to a doe. Actually, I wish I had a decoy that could sprout antlers by remote control so I could switch genders depending on the situation. If a dominant buck showed up alone, I would make the antlers disappear. If he showed up with a hot doe, I'd pop out the antlers and threaten his position in the pecking order. I don't rattle at this time because, in my experience, it makes weary does run like the wind. I don't grunt much, either, because I've found that bucks don't care as much about other bucks at this point. The best advice is to spend as much time in the woods as possible.

DESPERATION PHASE

Now we're getting into mid- to late November. The majority of the does have been bred and are getting back together with their fawns. They're preparing for winter by packing away the calories. But the bucks' breeding desires have not been packed away just yet. In fact, desperation sets in, and they are looking anywhere and everywhere for a doe that may have slipped through the breeding dragnet. Some does come into estrus late, and bucks of all sizes and shapes are still in the mood.

During one rutting season, I had a particular buck close twice when he'd been corralling a hot doe on a small riverside ridge, but I had never gotten a shot. A week later, after he'd bred his doe, I got another chance. I was using a doe decoy, and the instant the buck spotted it, he walked through seventy-five yards of woods like he was on a mission. Had I not slipped an arrow between his ribs from twenty-two yards away, he'd surely have broken the back legs on my decoy. That buck was so skinny from the rut that he didn't have a piece of fat bigger than my thumbnail on his body. He was desperate, and it cost him dearly.

Strategy: If I'm still-hunting at this time of year, I'm also desperate. I spend lots of time in a tree, trying to be there when things are happening. I still use my doe decoy, but I don't rattle and seldom grunt because the deer have probably heard it all by now. I hunt heavy trails leading to feeding and bedding areas and hope a late doe or fawn brings a desperate buck by.

LEFTOVER PHASE

The seventh phase is the leftover phase. It's a time when some early-born fawns come into estrus and unbred does come into their second cycle. This is the time when you will see a large buck standing in an open field with what appears to be a fawn. It could occur in the middle of the day and right at the edge of town. A dozen years ago, we had a huge seventeen-point non-typical hanging around my hometown. Everybody knew about him, but no one had gotten a crack at him during the bow or gun seasons. There were three days left in the gun season when I happened to spot the huge buck in the company of a fawn at noon in a field adjacent to our airport. I wasn't hunting, but as I watched, another hunter spotted him and it was over quickly. The buck lost his life worrying about "leftovers."

Strategy: Most deer are focused on the food supply, and so am I. I also scout a bit more, looking for a buck that's not getting hunted. If I find one, I try to hunt on my feet, taking advantage of quick setups and even ground blinds.

Those are my thoughts on the whitetail rut. They are more opinion than fact, but then, so are most theories on animal behavior. And I also have plenty of unanswered questions. I suppose that if I knew it all, I'd be killing a big buck every year, but that isn't happening. I'm just a bowhunter trying to understand the animal I seek.

I have as much fun at that as I do during what I always hope is the final phase of a hunt: wrapping my hands around the antlers of a buck and grinning for the camera.

7

THE EZ GUIDE TO CALLING BUCKS

by Michael Hanback

Need to know what call to use and when to use it?
Here's a quick and easy guide to various calls.

During the last few years you've probably read hundreds of articles on grunting, bleating, and rattling. Cable TV shows and videos have examined every nuance of calling deer. Biologists and wildlife managers have thrown in their two cents worth. By now you might have sensory overload. You might be thinking, "Maybe rattling and grunting really are rocket science."

Not true! The keys to the game are actually simple: (1) choose rattling, grunting, and bleating devices that sound good to you; (2) have confidence in those calls; (3) put 'em to work during the three distinct phases of the rut.

Here four experts offer some solid and straightforward tips to help you ring up a buck this season.

WILL PRIMOS
(PRIMOS HUNTING CALLS,
JACKSON, MISSISSIPPI)

Favorite Calls:

- Primos Power Buck and Doe (grunt/bleat call)
- Model 711 Easy Estrus Bleat
- Fightin' Horns (synthetic rattling antlers)

Pre-Rut:

Many days I grunt every fifteen to twenty minutes on stand. I want deer to hear me and come to hunt me. When the big-time scraping begins and bucks become increasingly aggressive I grunt, some-

Will Primos with a buck he grunted in during the pre-rut. (Photo courtesy of Bob McNally.)

times snort/wheeze, and then rattle for ten to fifteen seconds. I lay down the horns and keep still. A buck will sometimes come for a peek.

The ideal situation is to see a big deer or hear him walking in the leaves. I grunt at a buck to get his attention. I follow up grunts with one to three stressful bleats, like a doe coming into estrus. Mimicking a breeding scene like that has worked great for us the last few years.

Peak Rut:

It's tough to call bucks when they're hot on does, either chasing or breeding them. But I keep calling. You never know when a big deer will lose a doe. Or you might catch a mature or subordinate buck cruising around between does. I keep grunting and estrus bleating. I rattle occasionally to strike a buck that just parted ways with a doe.

Post-Rut:

Most bucks are skinny and worn out from rutting, especially late in the season. The last thing they want to hear is a lot of loud rattling, grunting, or bleating. My strategy now is to set up near a food source and blow soft "contact" grunts every once in a while. Just try to sound like another deer taking it easy and feeding. You never know when a buck might come to investigate.

Best Tip:

When a buck hears your rattles, grunts, or bleats he begins to hunt you. So your stand had better be in a spot with cover. If it isn't a buck will look down through the woods, see no doe or fighting bucks and then hang up out of range. Hide your stand in a tree with thick ground cover around it. Make a buck walk close in search of the "deer" he hears.

Harold Knight recommends calling or rattling during a new moon prior to the rut.

HAROLD KNIGHT
(KNIGHT & HALE GAME CALLS, CADIZ, KENTUCKY)

Favorite Calls:

- Knight & Hale Magnum Grunter
- Two Bucks in a Bag (6-inch rattling bag)

Pre-Rut:

This is an exciting time to call because deer are all fired up. But I don't just walk into the woods and start rattling and grunting. I wait until I see deer moving a lot, going into that breeding mode. Then I set up on ridges or in edges with good cover. I rattle and grunt loudly and aggressively, often mixing the two calls. A lot of noise can pull a lot of bucks into range.

Peak Rut:

I don't rattle much if at all when bucks are chasing and breeding does, but I still grunt a lot. You might catch a big buck cruising around between does. This is a good time to grunt in what I call a "perimeter" buck—a subordinate that stands 150 yards or so away and watches a mature buck breed a doe. A perimeter buck is fired up and looking for action, so he might zoom over to check out some doe grunts. A subordinate buck might not have the biggest rack, but he might be a fine eight-pointer that you will gladly shoot.

Post Rut:

Overall, deer are less active now as compared to the pre-rut and, of course, the peak, although some mature bucks still prowl for estrus does. I go back and rattle and grunt from stands that I hunted in late October and early November, especially stands located in cover near the best scrape lines. That's where you're apt to call in a buck looking for one more doe to breed.

Once the rutting activity is over, I stop rattling altogether and tone down my grunting.

Best Tip:

In the last few years we've discovered that the new moon prior to the normal peak of the rut in an area is an excellent time to call. Bucks shift into breeding mode, if only for a few days. They're active

Brad Harris with a nice buck he took in the post-rut period.

and ready to mate. This can be the best time of the season to rattle or grunt in a big deer.

BRAD HARRIS
(LOHMAN GAME CALLS,
NEOSHO, MISSOURI)

Favorite Calls:

- Lohman Monster Buck
- Lohman Rattle Box

Pre-Rut:

When bucks just begin to rut in October, I play off that. I call fairly often from a stand, but I'm far less aggressive than I'll be during the peak of the rut in November. I spar with my box and blow mid-range contact grunts. I call blind and to deer that I see.

Peak Rut:

When bucks get active and aggressive late in the pre-rut and into the chase stage I crank up my calling. I rattle hard. I grunt and sometimes bleat loudly. On stand I blind call at least twice an hour, sometimes more. It depends on how many deer I'm seeing. When rutting bucks move all day, I call all day. One more thing: I really like sharp, high-pitched grunts and rattles. Rutting bucks seem to respond best to those types of calls.

Post Rut:

It's important to read the mood of bucks during this phase. Some bucks are still wired and looking for does, and they'll come to hard rattling and grunting. But the body language of other bucks tells you they are worn out and wary. To have any chance of calling in skittish deer you need to tone it down. Blow a few soft contact grunts.

Best Tip:

Call with the tempo of the woods. On days when birds and squirrels are active deer probably will be, too. Rattle and grunt a lot, within reason, and do it confidently. But on mornings and afternoons when the woods are dead the whitetails might not move much. Call less frequently and aggressively.

DAVE STREB
(QUAKER BOY GAME CALLS,
ORCHARD PARK, NEW YORK)

Favorite Calls:

- Quaker Boy Pro Grunt Master

- Bleat 'n Heat
- Quaker Boy Rattle Bag

Pre-Rut:

Early in the season I don't blind call a lot, especially when I'm bowhunting around a hot food source. Deer are coming to the feed anyway, so why call? On the other hand, if the deer activity is really slow for a couple of days, why not do a little sparring or grunting? You might make something happen.

I've had exceptional luck with doe bleats early in the pre-rut. Mostly I bleat in does, but you never know when a buck will follow them in.

Peak Rut:

Late in the pre-rut and on the verge of the peak, when bucks are feeling their oats and looking for does, I call more aggressively. I increase the frequency and volume of rattling and grunting. And I keep bleating, turning up the intensity to sound like an estrus doe.

Post Rut:

Bucks expend so much energy during the pre-rut and especially the peak. I think that most deer just want to take it easy when the show is finally over. I go back and hunt stands near food sources, zeroing in on areas with lots of doe activity. And I go back to calling like I did early in the season. I keep things soft and simple, grunting every once in a while on days when I feel the need to make something happen.

Best Tip:

Many hunters hang treestands anywhere in the woods and start rattling and grunting like crazy. To me that is a mistake. I think that where you call from is the key. Play the wind and set up near food sources, in cover with fresh rubs and scrapes, or in funnels with doe trails. The point is, rattle, grunt, and bleat in high-use deer areas. Sooner or later a buck should come calling.

8

BEST STANDS FOR THE RUT

by Bill Winke

The key to selecting stand sites is to focus on things you know about rutting bucks and forget your hunches about individual deer.

One truth about the rut must stick in your mind: It isn't orderly or understandable. When I first started hunting big deer during the rut, I thought good hunters should be able to figure out what a buck would do next.

Heck, bucks leave sign for everyone to see. That should be enough, right? I soon learned those bucks don't play by the rules. They're scam artists. Their sign doesn't enlighten. It misleads. They're playing with our heads, laughing as we bumble through their world. Well, maybe they aren't that devious, but it seems they give con men a run for their money. Trying to make sense of the rut produces only frustration. It became obvious to me that I didn't know the combination to the safe that held their secrets. How can we hope to predict where a buck will go next when he doesn't know himself?

It was like taking three jigsaw puzzles, mixing all the pieces together, and trying to create one picture using all of them. Finally, I started looking for a simpler approach. I sought the big picture and the fundamentals of buck movements by focusing almost entirely on cover and terrain. That's when things started to make sense and hunting started to be more fun. That's also when I started getting

By studying aerial photos you can pick out cover-related funnels between good doe bedding areas and identify likely creek crossings.

shots at the kind of deer I'd been looking for all along. That 3,000-piece jigsaw puzzle was reduced to a six-piece children's version. In an effort to do things by the book, I had been making the game too complicated.

KEEP IT SIMPLE

It's easy to lose faith in a game plan that relies on too many assumptions. Deer behavior isn't predictable enough for us to script a fancy plan. There's a lot of luck involved, and a lot of stand time. Simple solutions are best. They're easy to understand, easy to apply, and easy to believe in when things don't go well. The key is to base your strategies on things you know for certain about bucks during the rut, and forget about guesses and hunches involving individual deer.

If you're sitting over a scrape and no buck shows up, it's tempting to think about finding a different scrape. But when you hunt fundamental travel patterns that all bucks use during the rut, it's much easier to focus and stay on stand. Simple stands instill enough confidence to keep you plugging along until the moment everything comes together.

The simpler-is-better philosophy requires we know one basic characteristic of all bucks during the rut: Bucks look for does in the places where they bed. After scouring one bedding area, bucks move to the next. Therefore, the best rut stand for most hunters is a funnel between two bedding areas used heavily by does. These bedding areas should be within a quarter-mile of each other to cut down the angles and to make it easier to predict the best stand locations.

HOW TO FIND DOE BEDDING AREAS

Doe bedding areas can be found three different ways. The best way is to study sign after the season. A doe bedding area will have multiple beds in close proximity because does tend to bed in family groups. Bucks tend to be more solitary, at least after the bachelor groups break up in late summer. Look everywhere, but the most likely places are elevated points and ridges, islands in swamps, and areas with thick cover.

Second, you can usually find possible bedding areas from aerial photos and topographical maps. Again, focus on raised terrain and thick cover. These can be found with some map study.

Finally, you can go out during the season and walk a lot of ground. If you keep your noise to a minimum you can get close enough to see deer stand and run off. Of course, you've just spooked every doe in your area and likely busted a buck or two along the way. Doing it once won't cause irreversible damage, but this should be a last-resort method.

TYPES OF FUNNELS TO SEEK
BOTTLENECKS AND INSIDE CORNERS

Rutting bucks might seem more vulnerable, but they aren't stupid. When traveling, they stay close to cover so they can melt into the woodwork at the slightest hint of danger. As a result, they're somewhat predictable in how they relate to cover. Any place between two doe bedding areas where the cover narrows is likely to be a funnel for rutting bucks. There might not be a trail or even buck sign in these places because bucks don't leave much sign in places they merely pass through. But don't sweat the small stuff. The bucks will be there.

Good examples of cover-related rut travel routes are brushy fencelines between two woodlots, the inside corner of a field separating two thickets in one large block of timber, the places along an open ridgetop where fingers of cover from opposing slopes come the closest together, the outside bend of a creek or riverbottom separating cover in two adjacent inside bends, and so on. By studying aerial photos, you can see dozens of cover-related funnels in your hunting area. All you need to do is pick the ones between two doe bedding areas, and you're set for action.

Anytime you can find a creek separating two places where does like to bed, you have a dynamite ambush site.

CREEK CROSSINGS

Creek crossings create excellent funnels that concentrate traveling bucks. Deer don't like to swim when they can walk, and they don't like to climb or descend steep banks if a short detour brings them to more gradual slopes. Low-bank, shallow-water crossings are some of the best deer funnels. Deer also travel creek banks, bringing a second travel route into range of any stand near a creek crossing.

Crossings can be spotted by studying aerial photos. Look for S-curves in a stream or river. The flat part of the S—between the two curves—will almost always have a deer crossing. The tighter the curves in the S, the higher the cut banks and the more the deer are forced to use the shallow crossings in between.

If you're lucky, the creek flowing through your area is shallow. By autumn, even most year-round streams run low. You can often walk down the bottom of the creekbed to the base of the tree that holds your stand. Staying below the surrounding forest floor has its advantages. Deer can't hear or see you unless they're on the bank above. And by walking in the water, you don't leave ground scent to put deer on red alert.

Anytime you find a creek separating two places where does like to bed—which is a typical situation in broken country—you have a dynamite ambush site. Bucks pass through any convenient crossing. Look for stand locations where you can cover a heavy crossing and a trail paralleling the creek bank. Crossings that are the farthest apart will be used the heaviest and are the best choices. Set up downwind of the crossing and only hunt the stand when winds blow your scent at an angle over the creek.

DITCH CROSSINGS

The typical ditch starts at the top of the slope as a swale and possibly extends into a ridgetop field. As the swale cuts down the slope, it becomes an erosion ditch that grows deeper and steeper. Deer that are not pushed seldom cross a deep ditch because easier crossings are usually nearby. Thus, the funnel is often obvious.

Erosion ditches produce excellent funnels for the rut and are found everywhere terrain is broken. Deep, steep ditches make better funnels than ditches with gentle slopes. By the same token, ditches with long stretches between crossings are also better because they create more concentrated funnels.

It makes no difference where deer are going or where they're coming from. All you must know is that deer are in the area and the ditch lies between two bedding areas used by does. This simplifies the scouting. You don't even need to walk new ground to identify potential ditch funnels. All it takes is a talk with the landowner. That's not a lot of effort to invest when you consider that ditches are some of the best sites on any property.

It's typical to find a draw between adjacent points, because that's how the points formed in the first place. When the draw carries sufficient runoff, it will form a ditch. Not every draw between two bedding ridges will have a ditch in the bottom, but it's worth finding those that do because they're the best pinch points for buck traffic during the rut.

As bucks trade back and forth from one doe bedding area to the next, they will detour around the ditch. If you play your setup right, that brings them past your stand. In other words, you're seeking ditches between two bedding areas that are deep enough to influence buck travel patterns. Find such setups, and you have a killer spot.

SETTING THE TRAP

Now you must decide which funnels to hunt. The wind will answer that question. Examine the landscape to figure out if the wind will swirl. Wind usually plays tricks anytime you set your stand in a protected pocket of dead air. For example, when winds blow over a ravine, they swirl because the air in the ravine isn't moving as fast as the air above it. If your stand is in the bottom of the ravine, your scent washes back and forth.

Anytime you hunt an area with swirling winds, you're taking a big chance of educating deer and burning out your hunting area. You might get lucky, though, and tag a big buck when the wind is just right. I've gotten away with it a few times, but more likely, every nearby deer will bust you because your scent is impossible to miss as it swirls back and forth. (This is what happens most of the time I hunt such stands.)

Unless you have unlimited good spots to hunt, avoid situations where you risk educating deer. It's guaranteed to happen sooner or later in places where you can't control your scent. Of the three types of funnels described above, creek-crossing and ditch-crossing stands have the most potential to be wind risks.

As you walk a ditch toward the top of the slope, the last good crossing closest to the top offers the most consistent wind, and is the best choice for a stand. Again, this is the top of the ditch itself where deer are forced to go around. When looking at a creek crossing, determine if the entire creekbottom is dead air. If the draw it runs down is less than a quarter-mile wide from ridgetop to ridgetop, swirling winds likely rule the creekbottom.

AWESOME ACCESS

One thing all great bedding-to-bedding stands have in common is foolproof access—and all three of the stand locations described offer that. When you hunt a ditch, start in the valley and walk up the ditch to your stand. When you hunt the creek, walk in the water or along its edge. Most cover-related funnels are far enough from bedding areas that you can get in and out without bumping deer. You might have to come in from the backside if it borders a feeding area deer often use in the morning.

Ditches and meandering creeks are usually littered with dead-falls, so you should go in during the off-season with a chainsaw and clear a path. I have a spot where I hacked through a half-mile of ditch. It took me eight hours to do the job, but that ditch is the perfect low-impact avenue in and out of that area.

WHEN TO HUNT THE STAND

Bedding-to-bedding funnel stands can be productive any time of day and should be considered all-day stands during the rut. If you must pick a time, mornings are better than afternoons. If you don't want to stay on stand all day, consider an afternoon stand nearer food sources and move there after midday. Don't leave too soon, because the biggest bucks often travel these funnels late in the morning.

If you struggle to make sense of all the buck sign you find each fall, take heart. There is a simpler way to hunt deer. Forget the sign. Forget about patterning deer. Look for terrain and cover features that predictably influence deer movement. These are great spots for taking trophies. No pattern is easier to find and hunt than a funnel between two doe bedding areas. Make these stands the bedrock of your rut-hunting strategies.

9

CALLING THE RUT

by John Weiss

Hunters have been grunting up a storm for many years, but during the rut you'll see far more action if you find and call does instead.

When it comes to trophy deer hunting, there is a parallel analogy to big-bass fishing. To successfully catch lunker bass, there are really only two basic approaches. Either you go on a search-and-find mission with an arsenal of lures or you sit patiently and rely upon bait to bring the fish to you.

The same *modus operandi* applies to mature whitetail bucks, except that it's far more difficult to find them. This is mainly because they number so few in relation to the overall deer population. Plus, they range over a large territory and are among the most wary creatures on the planet.

However, whitetail bucks have an Achilles heel—the onset of the rutting season. As fall begins to blend with winter, nature once again issues her millennium-old decree for whitetails to propagate their kind by bringing does into receptivity while simultaneously flooding the bucks' endocrine systems with testosterone. Where do you think the term "horny" came from, anyway?

Of late, many accomplished hunters are beginning to drift away from the usual methods of calling rutting bucks by using grunt calls exclusively. Instead, they're taking a page from the bass angler's notebook and using bait. And what better "bait" could there be than a hot doe?

WHERE THE DOES ARE

Does are relative homebodies compared to bucks. So once you're in "doe country" during the rut, the second part of the equation is to call those does to your stand location, knowing full well that amorous bucks are sure to follow.

One way in which does are far more predictable than bucks is their greater daily need for water throughout the year. Their body metabolisms are more complicated because of the need to nourish twin fawns when they are still in the womb and then after parturition the need to produce milk for six to eight weeks. Following weaning in mid- to late summer, a doe continues to require a high-water intake as she enters a stress-recovery period that stretches into the fall and early winter months.

As a result, a hunter's first lesson in learning where to expect to find the greatest concentrations of does is to keep in mind what I like to call "the water factor." Especially during dry years, does like to congregate in the lower elevations where there are rivers, streams, drainage tributaries, and lakes.

Don't misunderstand this to mean that does remain inextricably tied to a source of water all day, every day. Instead, such sources of water tend to form the nucleus of their habitat. Naturally, there-fore, such locations are the best places to begin scouting for trails and other indications of their daily activities.

Conversely, since does are also able to ingest water from the vegetation they eat, by dew-licking during the night hours, and by drinking from random puddles and ditches, an unusually wet season

The weak link in a buck's armor is nature's decree that he breed. The rut is the one time of year he's most likely to become careless.

will see them steadily drifting farther and farther away from the bottomlands and into the uplands. Under these conditions, a hunter has little alternative but to resign himself to more scouting.

FINDING DOE TRAILS AND BEDDING AREAS

Just like male and female humans, some does and bucks have big feet and some have little feet. Therefore, tracks will often lie to you.

But there are several characteristics of deer tracks that are fairly reliable indicators of the sex of the animal that left them. Generally, a mature buck has larger tracks than a mature doe, and they are of greater width to support a buck's wider body trunk.

However, a much more telling find is discovering one or two relatively large sets of tracks accompanied by several sets of very small imprints, as this is a clear indication that one or two does are being followed by their most recent offspring.

Of course, the importance of this insight lies in the fact that during much of the year does use their own particular trails, as do bucks. But at the onset of the rut, as does begin entering their estrus cycles, bucks engage in what biologists refer to as "transference." This means they temporarily abandon their own trails and begin using those traveled by does in order to monitor the growing stages of sexual readiness in the females.

So, as strange and contradictory as it may sound, being able to identify doe trails during the rut is more likely to be helpful in collecting antlers than watching a so-called buck trail.

It's also beneficial to locate doe bedding areas. During the rut, does are not as sexually energized as bucks and continue to spend most of the midday hours in their usual bedding locations. Yet bucks tirelessly roam at all hours of the day, searching for ready females by scent-checking doe trails and patrolling female bedding areas downwind.

Doe bedding areas are easy to recognize. First, you'll see doe trails (with large and small tracks) entering thickets. And within the inner confines of the cover you'll find a multitude of matted ovals in the grass and snow-skiff; as with tracks, some of the beds will be moderately large in size and nearby you'll see smaller beds previously occupied by each doe's current offspring.

BLEAT CALLS THAT BRING IN BUCKS

Rudimentary fawn-bleating calls have been on the market for a number of years, although it was Harold Knight and David Hale—founders of the famous Knight & Hale Game Call Company—who pioneered the development of a fawn call that was far superior to anything previously available. But their fawn-bleating call came about quite by accident.

"Over the years we had received numerous requests from coyote hunters for a call that would bring the predators in close," Harold Knight explained. "Since young deer play a major role in the diets of coyotes, we collected tape recordings of actual deer bleating sounds from a fawn that was caught in a fence. Then we designed a call to duplicate those bleating sounds."

"Yet disappointed coyote hunters began complaining to us," according to David Hale. "They said the call brought in more deer than anything else! That gave birth to our EZ-Deer Bleat Call."

Curiously enough, the Lohman Manufacturing Company, another producer of quality-made calls, also experienced a unique twist during the development of its Deer Bleat Call.

"In our case," Brad Harris says, "hunters everywhere are having terrific success calling in deer, but those hunters living west of the Mississippi are enjoying an added bonus in that their use of the Deer Bleat Call is also bringing in antelope!"

In the animal kingdom—which includes domesticated animals as well as wildlife—females that have given birth at least once feel a maternal, instinctive need to protect the young of their species, even if a particular individual is not their own.

"One time I was sitting in a treestand," David Hale explained, "and from about 250 yards away I was watching a doe with two yearlings by her side, which I am sure were hers. When I bleated with my call, she immediately threw her head up high and became alert as she looked straight in my direction. When I bleated a second time, she left her two young ones and charged straight toward me on a dead run, even though the distress call I was mimicking couldn't have been from one of her own."

But how does this apply to taking a buck? Well, as a doe begins to enter her estrus cycle, she emits hormonal pheromones that attract bucks and tell them she is about ready to allow breeding to take place. Naturally, a buck wants to make sure he is right there when she finally gives the go-ahead signal. Biologists refer to this behavior as a "tending bond" and the only way to separate a buck from a near-estrus doe at this time is by greatly alarming both deer and causing them to madly dash off through the woodlands. Even then, the buck will quickly make a wide circle and then frantically zigzag back and forth in an attempt to locate the doe's scent trail and reunite with her.

Obviously, during this peak of the rutting period, it is virtually impossible to call a buck away from a hot doe by rattling antlers or using a conventional grunt call. Both of those techniques are best reserved for the pre-rut, several weeks before does begin entering the first stages of their estrus cycle.

Faced with this frustrating situation, most hunters either throw their hands up in despair or continue to futilely grind away with their antlers and blow on their grunt call. Yet there's an easy solution at hand.

Simply put, since it's nearly impossible to use a call to get a rut-crazed buck to break his tending bond with a doe in heat, just call

Brad Harris was one of the pioneers of using a bleat call to lure in bucks. (Photo courtesy of Lohman Game Calls.)

the doe instead and you can be sure the buck will tag along right behind her.

"Even though a doe might be at the very zenith of her estrus cycle and is repeatedly being serviced by an amorous buck, she still feels the maternal instinct to come to the assistance of a fawn or yearling she perceives to be injured or suffering from some other distress," Brad Harris explains.

"If I were allowed to take only one type of calling instrument on a deer hunt, and had to make a serious choice, I'd probably pick a bleat call such as our Fawn Bleat," Will Primos, of Primos Hunting Calls, recently said to me. "The reason is because the effectiveness of antler rattling and using grunt calls is restricted to a fairly narrow time frame during the early rut-preparation period. Moreover, only bucks respond to these two particular calling methods. Yet a bleat call can be used anytime of year to bring in both does and bucks."

TALK THE TALK

Many serious deer callers joke that the only thing you can do wrong with a bleat call is not use it. Nevertheless, there are a few tips that will make any bleat-calling effort far more effective.

If you're sitting in your stand and there are no deer anywhere in sight, blow on the call about ten or twelve times every twenty minutes. Don't blow more frequently than this because on a calm day deer can hear this call up to a half-mile away, and even if they respond immediately it will take them a bit of time to travel the distance.

"If no deer are in sight," Harold Knight advises, "blow your call as loudly as possible. Don't be shy about really putting on some theatrics with a lot of intense wailing. If you've ever heard a live fawn or yearling when it was caught in a fence or being pulled down by a coyote, you already know that it screams its lungs out, and that's the very intensity, volume, and pain you want to project with your call."

"But if you have a deer in sight," David Hale adds, "don't blow as loudly. Tone the volume down by cupping your palm over the end of the call. But do continue to embellish your calling with plenty of distress cries and screams."

I would add another important point: Once you've made your calling effort, and you see a deer, and it's clear that the deer is responding to your call and coming your way, stop calling!

Once an animal has responded and is traveling in your direction, the call has performed its function, so put it down and let the animal search you out. Never lose sight of the fact that deer have the ability to accurately pinpoint the source of sounds they hear, so repeated calling on your part will only serve to make it easier for them to detect your presence. Conversely, if the deer has to hunt you, there is a greater chance it won't immediately peg your whereabouts, and this will make it easier to raise your bow or gun without being detected.

The only time I begin calling again is when a previously responding animal "hangs up" out of shooting range and refuses to come any closer or when a gusting wind causes a deer to become confused over where the call originated. Then and only then will I call very softly in an attempt to coax the deer toward me.

FINE-TUNE YOUR APPROACH

It's also worth saying that even though a majority of deer hunters nowadays use treestands, many hunters switch to ground-level blinds of sorts when using bleat calls because of the added realism they can give to their calling. Keep in mind that you are attempting to imitate a fawn or yearling in distress. And what could sound more real than blowing on your call and then violently rustling dry leaves with your boots so that you sound like an injured deer thrashing and flopping around? If you do elect to use a tree-stand, however, consider occasionally grabbing onto a nearby branch that is festooned with dry leaves and giving it a good shaking; but be forewarned that such blatant movement, especially when bowhunting, should be done only when there are no deer visible in the immediate area.

Since a properly used bleating call issues a piercing sound like a wailing banshee, many hunters might wonder if there are situations in which the call would actually spook deer.

"In all of the years that we've been experimenting with our Fawn Bleat calls, we've never yet had a deer register a frightened or alarmed reaction," Will Primos once explained to me. "In fact, usually just the opposite is true, and we can prove it.

"Our company does a lot of filming of deer behavior in hunting situations," Primos continued, "and we've got miles of footage showing does responding to bleat calls. In one video series we produce, titled *The Truth About Whitetails*, there is footage of does racing straight in our direction, passing directly beneath our stands, slamming to a halt, looking around, and trying to find the source of the bleating sound. Then another hunter, maybe seventy-five yards away in another tree, will blow on his call and the deer will run over there. Then, when I blow again, the animal reverses direction and comes right back to me again!"

Bucks, on the other hand, rarely charge in the direction of a fawn-bleat call. Generally, their reaction is to simply trail behind the doe, sometimes as much as 100 yards, with their heads held low in a cautious sneaking manner.

"When a doe is responding to your bleating, the way you can tell if a buck is likely to be following her is by reading the doe's body language," Brad Harris says. "When does are in estrus and know a buck is behind them, they extend their tails straight backward and tilted slightly off to one side, which is the universal signal they are ready to breed."

BE A WHINER

Another new doe-calling technique deserves mention. This is the estrus-doe bleat, or estrus-whine, which can be made with any fawn-bleat call to bring in amorous bucks any time during the pre-rut, peak-rut, or post-rut periods.

This particular call is not supposed to simulate a young deer that has been injured, so the hunter should not blow hard with a lot of intense, painful wailing. The effectiveness of this call is based upon the fact that within a local herd population not all does experience simultaneous estrus cycles. Some does, in fact, may go into heat as much as several weeks earlier or later than the majority of others. When this situation occurs, an estrus doe that is not already paired up with a tending buck will actually go looking for a mate, stopping periodically to make an estrus bleat in the hope of drawing a buck's notice.

Making an estrus-bleat sound with a fawn-bleat call is accomplished by blowing into the mouthpiece softly for several seconds duration, but with no dramatic, distressed rise or fall in the pitch of the sound. What you want to convey is merely a doe's sense of sexual anxiety with her characteristic high-pitched monotone pleading for company. And, naturally, a prime location to use this call is in the vicinity of scrapes, because a buck making his rounds is likely to hear the distant sound and be duped into thinking a doe has chanced upon one of his mating invitations and is anxiously awaiting his return.

"Even better than using a fawn-bleat call to make an estrus-doe whine is using an adjustable call such as our new 6-N-1 model," says Brad Harris at Lohman. "By means of an adjustable O-ring you can simulate hot-doe bleats or any of the five other vocalizations deer make without having to have numerous calls hanging around your neck."

This doe whine also simulates a lost-contact call that doe family units use to reunite when they become separated. In this case, however, when a doe is not yet in estrus and is being pestered by an amorous buck, she'll often try to dump him on another doe. If you sound like that "other woman," a nearby buck is likely to investigate in the hope that she is indeed in estrus.

At Primos Hunting Calls, their new Hardwood Fawn Bleat serves a dual function; it produces estrus-doe bleats and fawn-distress bawls. To my knowledge, Primos also markets the only deer "box call" on the market, called the Easy Estrus Bleat. Just turn the call upside down and back up for a perfect pleading doe bleat.

To be sure, none of these calling techniques are effective 100 percent of the time. Just keep in mind that the key time to use a fawn-bleat call to draw in a doe—and hopefully a trailing buck—is during the peak of the rut, but using an estrus-doe whine to purposely call in just a buck may produce results anytime from October through January.

10

JUST A MATTER OF TIME

by Kenn Young

The rut is universally known as the best time to harvest a really big whitetail buck, but hunting the rut can be an intricate puzzle unless you understand what happens and when.

E d Schwartz had seen a lot of unusual deer behavior over the years, but on this cold November day even Ed was having trouble believing the scene taking place in the overgrown field in front of him.

"My stand was in a large oak overlooking a good trail intersection," Schwartz explained, "there was a large sage field beyond that. But after I climbed into my stand that particular morning there were sounds like I had never heard coming from the direction of that old field. Wheezes, bawls, snorts, even shrill whistles, all combined with sounds I knew had to be deer running."

It probably should be mentioned here that Ed is a bowhunter, and one who makes even the term "fanatic" seem less than appropriate. His largest whitetail, a nineteen-point, non-typical taken in 1988, was for a long time the largest bow kill listed in the Arkansas Big Bucks Association record book.

"I go in early, two hours or more before even first light," Schwartz stated, "that lets the disturbed nightlife have time to calm down after my passing. I'm as careful as I can be, but no one can be completely quiet in the dark, so that extra time helps things get back to normal. I can tell you this; sitting there that morning in the total blackness that happens just before dawn, listening to those sounds, well . . . it was eerie.

"Finally it was light enough to make out what was going on in that field, and it sure was something to see. First a doe burst from the thick brush along the edge, running like the devil was chasing her . . . maybe he was from her viewpoint. Because right behind her, his outstretched nose nearly touching her tail, came a huge ten-point buck. A second later, another buck, a large eight-point, charged into the opening and raced after them. Then, not more than a second or two later, still another eight-point broke from the opposite edge and joined the chase!"

Schwartz paused for breath, his eyes alight at the memory, his voice actually quavering as he continued.

"For a good five minutes those three bucks chased that old doe around that field, it looked for all the world like some sort of furry train. Her tongue was hanging out and the bucks slung saliva with every step. Their grunts and wheezes were even more pronounced now that they were closer. After about five minutes, the whole group crashed back into the thick cover and disappeared out of hearing. They never came into range, and it was probably a good thing. I was

Forest openings are deer magnets until man's annual fall invasion forces a change in their movement habits.

shaking and sweating at the same time, my heart about to give out. I guarantee you, it was an experience I'll never forget."

It is a well-documented fact that the period we call the rut can have a drastic effect on the hunter's chances of taking a good buck. Without the sexual urge, which causes even the older bucks to occasionally let their guard down, prospects for success would definitely be far less. Where those oldest, most dominant bucks are concerned, not only is the rut the best time to hunt them, in many cases it is the only time.

Many hunters still believe the rut to be only that short period when the bucks are actually with the does. However, experts such as Drs. R. Larry Marchinton and Karl Miller of the University of Georgia School of Forestry Resources logically argue that the rut is actually composed of the entire period from velvet shedding until antler casting. This would encompass a total time frame of more than five months in most regions. During that entire period a buck undergoes gradual but continual changes, all brought about by the effects of his breeding urge. Knowledge of what is happening—but more importantly when it is happening—will certainly improve your hunting chances.

EXPLAINING THE RUT

From the hunter's viewpoint, there are four distinct periods within the overall rut time frame: (1) the early-fall period; (2) the pre-breeding frenzy; (3) the breeding period itself; and (4) the post-breeding period. Each of these offers hunting opportunities, but only to the hunter who is adaptable.

While the actual dates may vary for your particular area, the time frames should stay fairly uniform. But before we can utilize this guide, there are some popular myths and misconceptions that we must rid ourselves of.

As a youngster, I was taught by the old-timers that the rut was triggered by the first cold snap of the fall. Other tales have it being the first frost, or the first full moon, or even the rise and fall of the sap in the trees. While each of these may somewhat coincide with the rut, none have any real effect on breeding.

The breeding urge is brought about by photoperiodicity, the amount of light reaching the eye. Daylight naturally decreases in the fall and increases in the spring, due to the earth's rotation on its axis. Because this is an annual cycle, once you have determined the dates for your area, they will remain the same year after year. External factors, such as hot weather, intense hunting pressure, and out-of-balance buck-to-doe ratios may affect breeding intensity and visibility, but the actual times remain the same.

One single day, the peak breeding date, is the fulcrum of our whole rut diagram. That is the day when the most does are bred annually in any given area. It is important that you know the date for the *exact* locale in which you hunt, since it can vary slightly from one location to another. If you can't determine this date through actual in-the-woods observation, your state game department keeps extensive records on breeding activity and can pinpoint the date for you.

Once you know that date, it is simple to make a time-frame calendar of the various rut stages. Let's say the peak occurs around November 15, a somewhat common date throughout much of North America. One breeding period normally lasts ten to fourteen days, making the time frame approximately November 7 to 22. The pre-breeding frenzy (the brief period that provides the very best rut hunting of the entire year) takes place three to five days before that first doe reaches estrus, November 1 to 7. The long early fall period stretches backward from that point to the time of velvet shedding, which normally occurs during the first two weeks of September, so this period runs from around September 15 to November 1. On the other end of the spectrum, there is the post-breeding period, which lasts for about seven to ten days immediately after the breeding period ends—November 22 to December 1.

When completed, your calendar should provide an accurate visual guide to rut activity for your individual hunting area. While each period is a part of the overall rut, buck attitudes and activity during each time frame will be far different.

THE EARLY-FALL PERIOD

In early September, a burr forms around the antler base, cutting off the blood supply to the velvet. This formation is caused by a rise in testosterone, a form of steroid within the buck's blood, and is triggered by photoperiodicity.

The most visible effect of the testosterone increase is enlargement of the neck muscle. While many hunters still believe that a rutting buck's neck swells, that is not actually the case. The muscles enlarge primarily as a result of the buck "fighting" saplings, with testosterone enabling that build-up to occur at a rapid rate.

The rutting urge and subsequent activity during the entire fall is progressive. Early, the bucks are somewhat nocturnal and invisible, but their increasing desire and frustration gradually forces them to move more and more. I compare the males during the entire rut cycle to a clock being slowly wound tighter and tighter, and then suddenly allowed to unwind. The tightest point occurs during the pre-breeding frenzy, and this is when the most visible activity will occur.

Scrapes may be made as early as mid-September, but these are only boundary markings and seldom revisited. Rubs occur at almost any time and will often be evident even when scrapes are not. Scrapes are seldom found in some areas for the most basic of reasons; these pawed spots are advertisements, spots where bucks meet does. If there are high numbers of does in any area, the buck can pick and choose—he doesn't have to advertise!

I concentrate on travel routes during the early fall period, usually from an elevated platform. I start out hunting access trails to food and bedding areas, then switch to areas of scrape and rub concentration as November nears. I also search out doe areas during midday non-movement periods. Knowing these locations will become vital as actual breeding nears. Why? When the does are ready, the bucks will be with them.

THE PRE-BREEDING FRENZY

This brief period is without a doubt the most productive few days of the entire season for the knowledgeable rut hunter.

For roughly a week prior to that first doe reaching estrus, the bucks move far more often—their inner sex drives even causing them to occasionally prowl during daylight hours. Their attitude is now openly belligerent, and real fights can occur (not to be confused with the early fall shoving matches that hunters often see). They occasionally take "jaunts," long circular trips, during which they search for receptive does and in general just "go on the prod." They move closer to the doe areas, finding bedding spots in thick cover near the concentration zones. Rubs and scrapes are made and worked with increasing vigor. In short, particularly during the last few days before that first doe reaches estrus, even older bucks come close to being totally out of control.

Virtually any hunting method that is based on a buck's desire to breed may work at this time. Scrape watching is certainly at its most productive, as the bucks continually check for does. Remember that occasionally a doe, or even a subordinate buck, will stay in the immediate vicinity of a working scrape. Be careful on your approach to your nearby stand; nothing can ruin a day of hunting faster than spooking deer on your way in. When watching scrapes, doctor them with estrus doe urine, and never forget wind direction or become careless with your human scent.

Rattling will be effective, particularly in areas of high buck concentration. Inject violence into your technique; bang and grind the antlers together for periods of twenty to thirty seconds, stomp the ground, thrash underbrush and rustle leaves. All these are natural fighting sounds that bucks expect to hear. After you complete a sequence, give a few tending grunts and then wait, keeping your eyes trained downwind. In most instances, rattling is a two-man operation; the rattler and a shooter located 75 to 100 yards downwind overlooking dense cover. It is simply a buck's nature to check with his nose before he sees with his eyes. But never forget that the really dominant buck in that area may not care which two bucks are fighting. If his urge is high, he may simply walk in from any direction at any time.

One frosty December morning, I was rattling along the edge of a small pear flat on a well-known south Texas ranch. My companion was a dentist friend from New York who had never hunted with horns before, and he was more than a little skeptical of the whole idea.

He had just voiced that opinion for about the tenth time, low-voiced to be sure, when suddenly a buck neither of us had seen crashed through the surrounding brush within yards of our position. The large nine-point took one look at the two "does" and immediately reversed direction, actually kicking sand on us for good measure. The New Yorker, who tumbled backward into a patch of prickly pear as the buck nearly jumped over him, still considers rattling to be dangerous.

Scent canisters, 35mm film containers filled with unscented cotton saturated with estrus urine, will attract a buck when placed upwind of scrapes or bedding areas. Scents can work, if timed right and handled correctly. There can be nothing more exciting than listening to a large buck, grunting with every step, heading your way

Gerald Bethge with a monster. Many hunters regard the post-breeding phase as the hardest of the various rut periods to hunt. This is at least partially true because many bucks have been taken already, and the survivors are doubly wary and reclusive.

through the pre-dawn dimness. It can make even a veteran hunter's neck hair stand on end.

The frenzy is the one period when even old bucks are most likely to do unusual things at unusual times. This often makes the sheer amount of time spent in the woods the deciding factor in success. It's an old truism: "You can't kill him if you're not there." Take a lunch, water, and hunt from "can see to can't see." You'll have no better chance of killing a good buck.

THE BREEDING PERIOD

This period begins the moment that first doe reaches estrus. While it may not be the best time for the expert hunter, it is undeniably the period during which most really large bucks are taken.

Why is this true? Because bucks are doing something they do at no other time of the year; they are seeking out and breeding does.

Even the real oldsters sometimes lose just an edge of their caution, due to that overriding desire to breed. That explains why a few real monsters are taken each year standing in open fields, crossing busy roads, or in bare clear-cuts—definitely not your normal big buck spots.

Two things normally occur when a buck encounters a receptive doe. If he is the dominant buck of the area, and if no other bucks are following her, he will merely stay with her. In essence, he will briefly adopt her travel patterns, a change which can prove to be his undoing. Does seldom live in areas as thick and inaccessible as bucks and are not as cautious in their movements. This puts the buck in a precarious position when hunters are in the woods. If competition is heavy, he will try to herd her to a more secluded spot. This trait is naturally more common late in the breeding period when fewer does are available.

Normally he will remain with the doe until she passes out of estrus, twenty-four to thirty-six hours. When she loses her appeal he will immediately leave her and head for the nearest doe area, checking any working scrapes in the vicinity.

Scrape watching, rattling, and calling become something of a hit-or-miss proposition during the actual breeding period, at least for the bigger deer. The most dominant bucks will be with the does, leaving the scrapes and fights to the younger bucks.

Smart hunters become what amounts to doe hunters at this time, either still-hunting around doe areas or setting up stands along travel routes within them. Once again, the sheer amount of time spent in the woods becomes a primary ingredient in success. Even the most mature buck will occasionally do stupid things while under the rut influence, but you have to be there to take advantage of those momentary mistakes.

Three years ago, I nearly ran over a good ten-point standing within yards of a busy highway, at eleven o'clock in the morning, with cars passing almost under his nose. For a long minute, with brakes squealing all around him, he stood gazing into a field on the other side of the road. Finally he turned and walked unconcernedly back into the woods, but not before giving several passing hunters severe heart checks!

Why was he there? Although I never saw them (or even thought to look), I imagine there were does in that field across the road. Whatever the reason, for the briefest of moments he was preoccupied, and therefore vulnerable.

Slip-hunting, still-hunting, whichever term you prefer, can be very effective when hunting the breeding period, especially during windy or damp weather. Many writers today fail to recommend this hunting technique because few hunters do it well enough to be effective. But for those with the patience, easing through a doe area and maybe throwing in an occasional tending grunt can definitely pay some big dividends. While the breeding period may not be the best time for the more experienced hunter, it is without question the average hunter's best chance of harvesting a lot of horns. Once again, total time spent in the woods is often the deciding factor.

THE POST-BREEDING PERIOD

Many hunters regard the post-breeding phase as the hardest of the various rut periods to hunt. This is at least partially true because many bucks have been taken, and the survivors are doubly wary and reclusive. But as always, the successful hunter will be the one who understands and adapts his methods to what is actually taking place.

During the first two to three days after that last doe passes out of estrus, hunting may be similar to that of the pre-breeding frenzy; in a word, outstanding! The bucks are once again searching for nonexistent ready does. Try all the effective hunting methods of the frenzy; rattling, scraping, and scents. They will work, although for a far briefer time. The bucks have now been in perpetual motion for many long weeks and are just plain tired. When no available does are found, their interest quickly wanes.

Mother Nature has thrown her subjects a serious curve at this time. The combined pressures of the rut and hunting season have left the bucks in their poorest physical condition of the entire year. This at a time when they are looking the dead of winter—the time of lowest food availability—squarely in the face. Older males again become extremely reclusive, resting as much as possible, moving only to feed, and becoming completely nocturnal if there is even a hint of hunting pressure.

With the bucks in that reclusive state, the hunter must go to them to be effective. The places they retire to will almost invariably be remote and hard to hunt. Forced movement—drives, pushes, even dogs (where legal, of course)—may become the best alternative to flush a good buck from such heavy cover. Group hunting does not appeal to some, myself included, but late in the season it may well be the only way. Slow, silent drives by a small group of veteran hunters who know the terrain like the back of their hand can be deadly. Drivers and standers have about equal opportunity in most cases, because big bucks will lie close. You literally have to step on them to make them move. Even then there will be no wild, headlong flight through the woods: it's strictly out of sight and back into cover, the quicker the better. One trick of old bucks that have played this game before is to slip back through the drivers at some point within dense cover. Shots are generally close and safety should always be the primary concern.

Understanding rut chronology will certainly have a direct effect on your rut hunting success. Knowledge, and practical application of that knowledge, is the key. Your calendar illustration will work in virtually any area, the primary ingredient simply knowing the peak breeding date for that particular location. Once you have that one key, use or modify the various time frames listed to make your own guide. From that point it actually gets simple. You know what the deer are most likely to be doing, and you know when they will be doing it, often even before they do. Employ the correct hunting method(s) at the correct time, and you just may have the edge that will let you harvest your buck of a lifetime.

11

CLIMB HIGH FOR RUTTING BUCKS

by Bob Robb

There may be a lot of activity along lowland cropfields, but during the rut a good place to find some of the larger bucks is higher, along acorn ridges. Here's how to find them.

It was a typical November week of bowhunting for me. The green-fields were pockmarked with deer sign, including some very impressive buck tracks. There were several trails leading to and from the fields. And every morning and evening, I'd see a good number of does and yearlings feeding, with lesser bucks coming to scent-check scrapes and nibble on the alfalfa, winter wheat, and cutover corn.

Several days of this and my inherent wandering nature took over. After three hours on stand that third morning, I climbed down and headed off for a little walkabout. There were good bucks here. I could *smell* them. But where might they be?

I picked a large trail that began in the corner of a small field finger and began following it. Before long it started winding its way up a low hill, which led up onto a long acorn ridge. Whenever I found a bisecting trail that kept gaining altitude, I took it. Before long I was into some semi-steep stuff, before breaking out onto a large oak flat. I could hardly believe my eyes. Here there were trees the size of my thigh rubbed almost in half. Scrapes as big around as washtubs. Tracks that could have been made by a spike elk. And here and there, oaks that were still dropping acorns.

Be still, my heart! I eased along the edges of the flat, and by and by found some wide benches covered with thick brush and small trees. Ideal bedding thickets, they were, with trails leading in and out of them. The afternoon thermals were rising, keeping my scent blowing up and off the thickets, and with the muddy ground softened by recent rains, walking quietly was a snap. By and by I found what I was looking for—a big cedar trashed by a rutting buck, a fresh scrape not fifty yards away, and a fenceline crossing, all set in a small notch at the top of a hill. The spot was the junction of two deep cuts that led up from the thickets. If a deer came out of there and passed through this spot to the other side, it wouldn't have to travel more than a quarter-mile to the greenfields below.

It was about noon, and I couldn't get the climber stand hung fast enough. The day passed slowly. About 4 P.M., I caught some movement along the fenceline, and soon a 2½-year-old eight-pointer came to the scrape, worked the licking branch, then continued on. After three days of nothing, he was a pretty nice buck, but deep inside I knew he wasn't "da man." After he worked his way down the hill I settled in and got ready.

Nothing. That is, until ten minutes before slap dark. Down in the bottom of one of the cuts I caught some movement and wasn't really sure what it was. It came in my direction, heading right for the cedar, and soon the dark blob materialized into a dandy eight-pointer. I let him come, and when he walked behind a thick pile of brush I came to full draw. He stepped out the other side, head down as he made his way to the cedar. He never made it.

MOUNTAIN BUCKS

Few environments provide whitetails with more survival advantages than steep, mountainous terrain. For one thing, the steep, bluff country is physically harder for the average bowhunter to access. With so much deer sign in the lowlands near the majority of the late-season food sources, why climb high? The high country also provides the deer with a wide view of the area below, and they can see danger approaching. With the exception of dawn and dusk, the warm daytime thermal wind currents bring the scent of trouble wafting to them.

The high country is also an ideal place for an old loner buck to spend his days in the solitude he prefers. Here, where deer can live to 4½ years and more with regularity, they can avoid the scads of does, yearlings, and teenage bucks that live in their social groups on easier ground. They are not bothered by farmers and recreationists. When the rut comes, these bucks can easily access the lower country if no does are prevalent. However, there seem to always be a few does hanging around the high country, too. I doubt that many of these old monarch bucks have to travel far to find what they need.

When hunting mountain trails, don't bother setting up unless you find the sign of *big* deer. Oversized tracks are a good indicator that this is a great place to hunt.

HUNTING BEDDING AREAS

During the rut—when breeding is in progress, and after most scraping has been done—I like to hunt the high elevation bedding areas. This is not easy to do. They are usually small pockets of thick brush set in or near relatively open hardwoods, requiring the hunter to approach with great care.

In areas where humans farm the tops of the mountains, the bucks tend to bed a bit lower on the slopes, often in thickly wooded ravines or valleys near the heads of small streams. If there is no farming on top of the mountains, the bucks will tend to be nearer to the top, often with two types of escape routes close at hand—a steep slope directly below them or a steep slope located directly behind them, over the top of the mountain and down the other side. Again, thick woods or brush are where they prefer to lay up. In both cases, the areas will be far from roads that provide easy human access.

In addition to buck beds, you can also find doe bedding areas high in the hills. This is especially true in areas where hunting pressure is heavy in the lowland areas, when the deer are driven to live away from easily accessible areas. Of course, if you can find a pocket of does that will be in the same general area day in and day out during the rut, sooner or later Mr. Big will be there, too.

The key to hunting these areas is making a proper approach. I've found that the most direct route from a road is the least likely to be successful. That's because the bucks generally bed where they have a good view of these points, can monitor careless human movement, and get out of Dodge before trouble shows up. The best way to access these areas is a more circuitous route, widely circling the slopes directly below these bedrooms. When climbing, stick to cuts at least a quarter-mile away from where the deer are likely to be holding. This will keep them from easily seeing you, and the ravines will help funnel your scent up and away from them. When it's time to head for your stand site, take a trail that is above the bedroom, downwind, and beginning at least an eighth of a mile away. I hope to catch the bucks coming back to bed in the morning or leaving in the evening, but I've also caught them coming out at midmorning and mid-afternoon when the rutting urge overcomes their natural caution.

When trail hunting, don't set up your stand just because the perfect tree presents itself. Be on the lookout for big sign.

TRAIL HUNTING

On these high-country hunts I am looking for big bucks. That said, I never pick a trail to set up on unless it has big buck sign on it— big tracks, large droppings, or a rub line or large trees. I also look for trails taking the path of least resistance when traversing the mountains. Spooked deer may run straight up and straight down the slopes, but an unalarmed deer will generally travel a path that offers relatively easy walking. Studying the lay of the land or using a topographic map is a good way to locate potential travel routes.

I've also found that mountain bucks generally have just a couple of ways to approach a specific feeding or bedding site. Unlike their lowland brethren, who have an almost unlimited number of easy routes to choose from, in the mountains there are fewer easy options for travel.

Naturally, I like to find a trail that leads through a funnel like the one described earlier. Ravines, cuts, small saddles, creekbeds, and fencelines all act as natural funnels for buck movement to and

During the afternoons, deer tend to feed lower on the mountain, knowing the thermals will send dangerous scent down the slope to them. Benches with preferred foods such as persimmons located about a third of the way down the mountain are excellent evening stand sites.

from bedding areas. When scouting, I often look for funnels before I do trails, knowing that if I work a natural funnel eventually a deer trail will cross it.

THAT DAMNABLE WIND

Mountain winds are not like lowland winds. Up high, with steep bank edges, uneven edges, and tricky thermals, these winds can be as unreliable as a politician on the campaign trail. Your scent can be swept for a very long way up and down the mountain through natural funnels and ravines, along high ridges, and across open woodlots.

However, mountain areas usually have a prevailing wind direction that generally blows the same day in and day out. You can be sure bucks use these prevailing wind patterns to their advantage when choosing bedding locations. When you locate a potentially hot stand site, it is imperative that you set up according to the prevailing winds and morning/evening thermal current patterns. It is just as important that you avoid hunting these areas when the winds are wrong.

I grew up hunting high-country mule deer, so dealing with mountain thermals is really second nature to me. On calm mornings, thermals tend to waft scent up the slope, pooling it on high flats where bucks like to feed. On these mornings you will often find bucks concentrating their feeding efforts in these locations. Conversely, in the evenings the thermals will carry scent down the slope, pooling it on feeding flats off the tops of the mountains. That's where deer tend to feed in the afternoons.

Because mountain winds are as fickle as the proverbial finger of fate, maintaining a rigorous, no-short-cuts scent control program will up your odds immeasurably. I shower every morning with no-scent soap and launder my outerwear with no-scent laundry detergent, storing it in a clean plastic bag that I carry up the mountain in my daypack. When hiking the often long, steep route to my stand sites, I make sure I allow lots of time so that I don't have to push my body and force it to start perspiring. Once I reach my stand I cool down, then spray both my body and all my clothing items—undergarments included—with a no-scent spray.

I am a firm believer in the new scent-blocking outerwear technology. The past two seasons I've been wearing a jacket, pants, and cap featuring Gore's Windstopper Supprescent, and I believe it has helped me more than once from being smelled by deer who have wandered directly downwind of my stand. Some of my friends wear suits from Scent-Lok or ScentBlocker from Robinson Labs and like them, too. And for mountain hunting, you cannot beat the Gore-Tex Supprescent hiking boots from Rocky. They breathe, which helps wick sweat off your foot and out of the boot for maximum comfort, yet block 100 percent of human odor from escaping, just like rubber boots do. The pair I tested are designed just like mountain hunting boots, making hiking and climbing much more comfortable and safe than wearing knee-high rubber boots. They're ideal for this kind of hunting.

LET'S GO!

I hunt the mountains a lot today not because of the bucks I've killed there, but more for those that I have not shot. Here's an example, one of many stories I could tell you if we had an evening around the campfire.

Everything was perfect. I'd found the sign I was looking for—a rub line and trail leading up out of a wooded ravine and onto an oak flat. I found a way to access the flat from the opposite side of the mountain, and one calm morning made the two-hour hike to get there. I was able to make my way silently across the 100-yard-wide flat and got into my treestand without a hitch. As I settled in, it was hard to keep my heart from beating its way out of my chest. I just *knew* it was going to happen that day.

It did. Just a half-hour after first light a very, very large ten-point buck made his way up out of the ravine and headed my way. I was set up near a small saddle, and I just knew the deer was going to stroll right on through that saddle and down the other side. I thought I was calm, but I guess I was so focused on his chest that I forgot to look for little branches and such. When I released the arrow I knew he was mine. When, halfway to the buck, the shaft glanced off a branch and launched itself towards the moon, I felt sick to my stomach. I hunted that buck for two more weeks, and never saw him again.

No matter. It is encounters just like that that keep me hunting high-elevation whitetails. It can be hard work, and quite frustrating at times, but the rewards can also be big—as in Pope & Young big. Those kinds of bucks are more than worth the effort.

12

SURE CURE FOR THE POST-RUT BLUES

by Greg Miller

Hunting big bucks as the rut winds down can be an ordeal. Find the bedding area of one now, though, and you're on the doorstep to the buck of your life.

It seems I've been dealing with post-rut whitetails forever. In truth, my first go 'round with these difficult creatures took place in the Wisconsin Northwoods more than thirty years ago. As you might imagine, I've had more than my share of experiences with post-rut bucks since that first gun hunt with my dad way back in 1964. I've also been forced to deal with the situation many times during my home state's late archery season for deer. All these run-ins with post-rut deer have led me to formulate what I believe is a most accurate assessment. Achieving a consistent success rate on post-rut bucks is the most challenging endeavor facing modern-day whitetail hunters.

Many factors make hunting big bucks after the rut a tough ordeal. More than anything, however, it's the fact that bucks often adopt very reclusive lifestyles that puts hunters at a disadvantage. Instead of the carefree and careless attitudes displayed just days earlier during the rut, mature deer are now quite nocturnal and extremely man-shy. To our advantage, however, there is one thing that can force these otherwise skittish creatures to suddenly abandon their secretive ways—their ravenous post-rut appetites.

It's a well-known fact that while searching for receptive does rutting bucks don't take much time to eat. These self-imposed diets often last for three weeks or longer, depending on the length of the rut. As a result it's not unusual for the most active breeding bucks to lose up to thirty percent of their body fat. Particularly in northern regions, it's extremely important that big bucks replenish these exhausted fat reserves as quickly as possible. If they don't, and severe winter weather rolls in early, these bucks will be some of the first deer to perish.

My biggest bow-killed buck to date, a monster non-typical, was taken during the post-rut period. Unbelievably, I shot that deer while sitting on a stand located along the very edge of a snow-covered alfalfa field. A full hour before dark a half-dozen antlerless deer had wandered out to feed on the alfalfa. The does and fawns eventually made their way to within fifteen yards of my stand site. Some twenty minutes later I heard another deer approaching the field through the crusted snow. The next thing I knew a huge buck was walking straight toward my position. I had to wait several tense minutes for the buck to offer me a more suitable angle before I could take my shot. The eighteen-pointer took off across the field after the hit and made it nearly 200 yards before tipping over.

If you're not literally setting up on the doorsteps of buck bedding areas it's possible that you could hunt the entire post-rut period and not see a single antlered animal.

Taking post-rut bucks often entails far more planning and work than merely waiting in ambush near food sources, however. Hunters will realize more consistent results by setting up closer to bedding areas. The cumulative effects of weeks of hunting pressure and natural post-rut behavior will have led the bucks to adopt very restrictive movement patterns. These patterns see bucks leaving their bed-rooms right at last light in the evening and then returning to bed down at first light in the morning. In many cases if you're not liter-ally set up on the doorsteps of buck bedding areas, it's possible that you could hunt the entire post-rut period and not see a single antlered animal. Although I could cite many examples to help illus-trate my point, one in particular springs to mind.

I was sitting on a stand site that was situated a mere seventy-five yards from a buck bedding area. Approximately forty minutes before dark I noticed some movement near the edge of that bedding area. Seconds later a big buck stepped into view. Since it was still rela-tively early, I was confident the majestic animal would end up within bow range before legal shooting time expired. But it never happened. In fact, I doubt that big buck had taken more than a dozen steps when the clock finally ran out.

Trying to figure out exactly which runways are playing host to the greatest amount of buck traffic isn't all that difficult. I use the exact same approach when scouting during the post-rut as I use dur-ing the pre-rut period. Instead of picking runways at random, I con-centrate the bulk of my hunting efforts on trails that show the most rub activity. Since I prefer to limit myself to mature bucks, I look for runways that have the greatest number of large antler rubs.

Provided they have survived the many perils associated with the rut, whitetail bucks usually will return to their home ranges when breeding is finished. After resting for a couple days, the bucks will then get into the same food-related travel patterns they used earlier in the fall. Of even more interest to hunters, however, is the fact that bucks will use many of the same travel routes they used earlier during the pre-rut period. I should add that many of my best post-rut stand sites are located along pre-rut rub lines.

There's a reason why I like to spend my post-rut hunting time sitting in ambush along rub lines, and it's extremely important to keep this information in mind when deciding on post-rut stand locations. Whitetail bucks establish their rub lines along routes they feel are the most safe and secure. So in a way, they're actually telling you exactly where they most prefer to walk when traveling about their ranges. Because antler rubs are so highly visible during the late fall/ early winter period, it shouldn't take much time to find several potentially productive stand sites.

Just like during the pre-rut, concentrate the majority of your post-rut hunting efforts along active rub lines. Bucks establish their rub lines in areas where they feel the most safe and secure while traveling. A buck like this one could be the reward for picking the right setup.

I've stressed the point that post-rut bucks are notorious for moving only during first light and last light of day. For that reason, the majority of the stand sites I use at this time of year are placed in relative close proximity to bedding areas. Now I realize that some hunters have trouble figuring out exactly where the bucks they are hunting are bedding down. If it's any consolation, I used to struggle with the problem myself. That was often the case when I hunted unfamiliar ground. However, in recent years I've come up with a fairly effective way of dealing with the problem.

I start out by establishing stand sites along rub lines some distance back from the edge of known deer feeding areas. If I sit these stands a couple times without seeing any antlered activity, I'll then relocate farther away from the food and, hopefully, closer to a bedding area. I'll keep doing this until I either start seeing some bucks or decide I'm getting too close to where a buck is bedding.

What do I use as a guide to help me figure out if I might be getting close to a bedding area? In most cases, just plain old common sense. Severe changes in the topography of the land, sudden changes in the forest understory, or actually jumping deer from their beds can be clues that you're getting close to a bedding area or, heaven forbid, that you've already trespassed into one. If I have even the slightest suspicion that I'm nearing a bedding area, I'll stop right where I am and start looking for a stand site.

The non-typical I mentioned earlier abandoned his normal nocturnal lifestyle and showed up at the alfalfa field in broad daylight for one simple reason: A major winter storm was bearing down on our part of the world. No factor has a greater influence on post-rut deer movement than the weather. And be advised, this movement could just as well take place at literally any time during the night or day. From what I've seen, the absolute best time to be out in the woods is during the twelve-hour period leading up to the arrival of a winter storm. But hunting can also be quite good as a storm starts blowing out of the area. During these times, stand sites placed near to or right on the edge of feeding areas could be productive.

For the most part, I prefer to keep a silent vigil while hunting post-rut bucks. However, there are rare instances when I'll incorporate a bit of calling into my hunts. Usually, I'm prompted to try a bit of rattling and/or grunting because I've recently witnessed some secondary breeding activity in the area. I should add that my post-rut calling efforts are not anywhere near as aggressive as those I use earlier in the fall. For instance, I prefer to use rather subtle grunts. And instead of full-blown rattling sequences, I just mesh the antlers together and then slowly grind them back and forth for fifteen to twenty seconds. If a post-rut buck does respond to your calling, he will most likely do so in a very slow and wary manner.

Those who gun hunt during the post-rut period will find that the tactics I've already described could be very effective for them as well. However, there are a couple tactics for dealing with post-rut buck behavior that are exclusively suited to gun hunters. One of these tactics entails making small, three- to five-man drives through buck bedding areas. As with calling, I only recommend using the small drive method if the bucks you are hunting have adopted strict nocturnal movement patterns.

Here's how we do our small drives: After selecting an area, we send our standers into cover suspected as escape routes. (To keep from alerting the deer, these guys take extra care to keep from making any unnatural noises.) At a designated time, our drivers ease their way into the bedding area, keeping the wind at their backs. Hopefully, the bucks will smell these interlopers and slowly make their way out ahead of them. While we can't boast a high success rate, we do get a big buck to meander by one of our standers just often enough to make the tactic worthwhile. By the way, it should take only one or two drives through any bedding area to figure out exactly where fleeing bucks prefer to run. You can then post your standers accordingly on future hunts.

There's a reason why I'm so adamant about using a small group of hunters to make drives through bedding areas. It's much easier to keep your presence a secret when setting up drives where fewer hunters are involved. Post-rut bucks are extremely skittish creatures. In most instances they'll turn tail and run at the first hint of trouble. Keeping a low profile is a must. From what I've seen, that's nearly impossible to do with large groups of hunters.

Another post-rut gun-hunting tactic I'm particularly fond of entails putting up portable treestands to overlook buck bedding areas. I'm not talking about putting up stands on the edges of dog-hair thick spruce swamps or five-year-old regrowth areas. Rather, I'm talking about placing stands along the edges of more "open" bedding areas, such as grass swamps and one- to three-year-old clear-cuts. The great thing about this tactic is that you don't have to wait for the bucks to exit their bedding areas. Provided they are within range, you'll be able to drop them as soon as they stand up from their beds.

Several years back, during my home state's gun season, I used the aforementioned tactic to score on a post-rut buck. While I didn't actually see the buck stand up from his bed, thanks to three inches of noisy, crusted-over snow, I knew for a fact that he had taken only three steps prior to my shooting him. Actually, my attention was first drawn to the spot where the big deer appeared because I'd earlier heard a very suspicious, yet unidentifiable sound. (It took me a couple of days to figure out that it was the buck shaking himself like a dog.)

A FEW FINAL THOUGHTS

Due to the skittish nature of post-rut whitetails, I'd strongly recommend taking every possible precaution during this period. Personally, I take great pains to ensure that I'll be able to get to my stands sites without alerting the bucks I'm hunting. And to keep from putting too much pressure on any one buck, I constantly rotate my stand sittings. I absolutely refuse to sit a stand more often than once every three days at this time of year.

In addition, I shower and wash my entire body and hair with an odor-killing soap before each and every hunt. I also make sure my hunting clothes have been freshly washed in an odor-killing detergent and then line-dried. Finally, as is the case with all my deer hunts, I wear a Scent-Lok suit.

For those who might have trouble deciding if the post-rut period has begun, here are a few tips. One clue is a sudden and severe reduction in rub and scrape activity, but a more obvious and accurate clue is a sudden lack of daylight buck activity in and around known "rutting areas." If you don't see any chasing and/or breeding over a two- or three-day period, I'd say it's a safe bet the rut is over.

If you still have problems figuring out exactly when the post-rut occurs in your part of the country, I'd suggest contacting a wildlife biologist or game manager from your state's fish and game department.

I know many hunters who simply refuse to hunt during the post-rut period. The majority of these individuals cite reasons like a flighty deer herd and few buck sightings as the main reasons for this decision. I'm not going to lie. These factors can make for tough hunting conditions. But if you apply some of the techniques I've mentioned here I'm confident that your post-rut success rate will improve.

13

EARLY RUBS AND HOW TO HUNT THEM

by Greg Miller

If you thought that scrapes were misunderstood, try asking hunters about rubs. Here, once and for all, are the facts about early antler rubs.

There was a time when I hated the early part of the archery season—my hatred stemming from the fact that I had no clue how to figure out big bucks at this time of year. Oh sure, I knew all about doing the long-range observation thing in the weeks leading up to archery season. In fact, it was a rare occurrence when I hadn't spotted at least a half-dozen, shooter-size bucks prior to the opening of bow season. Figuring out where those bucks might be once opening day arrived, however, was another matter.

Then I happened to witness an interesting and informative occurrence while on one of my preseason observation trips. I had been watching a big buck as he grazed hungrily in a distant alfalfa field. After feeding for perhaps fifteen minutes, the buck strolled over to the edge of some nearby woods. He first sniffed and then licked a stout, forearm-sized sapling. The buck then lowered his head and did his best to destroy the little tree. He was still grinding away on the sapling with his huge rack when darkness fell a half-hour later.

It was while I was closely inspecting the antler-scarred tree a few days later that it suddenly hit me: Whitetail bucks did this sort of thing all the time! They made antler rubs all across their core areas throughout the entire pre-rut period. Further, from what I'd seen in the past, there usually was a spurt of rubbing activity just prior to opening day of archery season. All I had to do was figure out a way I could use this particular buck behavioral trait to my advantage.

I've spent a great deal of time throughout the past twenty years increasing my knowledge about buck antler rubs. There's no doubt in my mind that this increase in knowledge has made me a more successful trophy whitetail hunter. But becoming more knowledge-able has also made me aware that some obvious fallacies concerning antler rubs are still making the rounds. One of the most often re-peated of these has to do with early rubbing activity.

According to what some people would have you believe, the first rub activity that occurs is an indication that the bucks are in the process of removing their antler velvet. In reality, however, early antler rubs have very little to do with actual velvet removal. The first real flurries of rub activity are actually a signal that antler velvet has already been removed.

It takes very little time at all for bucks to remove the velvet from their antlers. In fact, the process sometimes can be completed in as little as thirty minutes, even by the largest-racked bucks. Another fact: In their attempts to remove antler velvet bucks often will do a lot of brush rubbing. (They push their antlers into a clump of brush and

In most cases, mature bucks will be stripped clean of their antler velvet before immature bucks. (Photo courtesy of Bob McNally.)

rub furiously.) Once the velvet is removed, however, bucks will then direct their rubbing attentions to saplings and small to medium-sized trees.

In most parts of North America, this first flurry of rubbing activity occurs in the days just prior to the opening of archery season for deer. Even more importantly, the vast majority of this rubbing activity occurs along routes the bucks are currently using and will continue to use throughout the first few weeks of the archery season. This last bit of information can prove to be extremely beneficial to early season bowhunters.

Before continuing, I think it's important to shed some light on several other key points regarding early antler rubs. To begin with, my research would indicate that the biggest bucks in a given area are usually the first animals to become rub-active. Also, big bucks usually make substantially more antler rubs during the early season than do immature bucks. Finally, big bucks won't hesitate to take on some very large trees immediately after velvet removal. Smaller bucks just don't seem to possess this same aggressive attitude—at least not during early fall.

As stated above, the majority of early antler rubs are found along the travel routes most often used by bucks at this time of year. However, bucks also display a propensity for doing a lot of early rubbing around the outside perimeters of preferred feeding areas. Although it's always nice to see these first buck signs suddenly appear, the importance of perimeter rubs as hunting aids is often overrated.

This is especially true when talking about mature bucks. Numerous past encounters with humans near food sources has resulted in big bucks everywhere developing mentalities that allow them to effectively deal with the situation. In most cases, they simply refuse to travel anywhere near a food source during daylight hours.

Still, those clusters of fresh rubs you find near food sources early in the season are proof positive that there are some bucks nearby. Just keep in mind that—in most cases—these bits of sign should be viewed as reference material only. You'll almost always realize a higher degree of early season success by setting up some distance away from the edges of feeding areas.

My good friend Doug Below has used his extensive knowledge of early antler rubs to ambush several large Wisconsin bucks. Doug agrees that big bucks usually become rub-active first.

"I've actually seen a number of smaller bucks that were still in full velvet on opening day of the bow season. But I've never seen a mature buck in velvet at that time," he told me. "Obviously, if the bigger bucks are shedding their velvet first, then they must be responsible for the majority of early rubs. At least that seems to be the case in my hunting areas."

Doug also agrees that early rubs can play a huge role in hunter success rates. "Hunters need to realize that whitetail bucks relate very strongly to their rubs, even during the early part of the bow season," he stated. "But it's equally important to remember that your best chance of ambushing a big buck will come from stand sites located along active rub lines some distance away from feeding areas."

Doug was quick to add that hunters should display extreme caution when scouting for rub-line stand sites during the early season. "I've noticed that big bucks have a tendency to bed somewhat closer to feeding areas at this time of year. I believe that the thickness of underbrush and foliage has something to do with this behavior. But whatever the reason, I'd recommend that hunters limit their initial scouting and hunting efforts to about a 200-yard radius from feeding areas. If you haven't seen any buck activity after a couple hunts, then move your stands farther back into the woods."

According to Doug there is another definite "perk" to be realized by hunting along early rub lines: "There have been numerous times when sitting along an early rub line has provided me with an opportunity to see every buck that was living within a particular core area. This is because the bucks are still pretty much in their bachelor groups at this time of year, and where one member of a bachelor group rubs, they all rub."

Doug cites the story about one of his best ever bow-killed whitetails, a massive twenty-one-point, non-typical, as a perfect example of early season bachelor group behavior. "It was the third day of the season, and I was sitting on a portable treestand I'd placed along a very active and distinct rub line," Doug told me. "Some time before dark, a small buck wandered by on the rub line. He was soon followed by another buck. Behind that buck was another. All told, there were five bucks in the bachelor group. As is usually the case, the largest buck, which happened to be the non-typical I arrowed, was bringing up the rear."

Doug also brought up an interesting point regarding the perimeter rubs I mentioned earlier. "There are those rare occasions when setting up near clusters of perimeter rubs could prove to be a productive tactic. This usually happens only if hunting pressure in the immediate area is relatively light. And even if this is the case, you'll probably only have a few days at the very beginning of the bow season when you can expect to ambush a big buck near a feeding area. After that you're going to have to relocate back into the woods a ways."

There's another benefit to be realized from becoming at least somewhat "literate" about early antler rubs. Not all bowhunters are able to get out during the preseason and watch the bucks they plan on hunting later on or, in some cases, do any intensive scouting. Believe me, acquiring a basic understanding of early rub behavior can provide bowhunters with a way to overcome these negatives.

The preseason scouting regimen I've come up with isn't complicated. It does entail doing a bit of legwork, though. I walk around the entire outside perimeter of a suspected feeding area, all the while keeping my eyes peeled for fresh antler rubs. Although I make a mental note of the location of any perimeter rubs I find, the primary focus of my search lies in another direction. In most cases I'll turn my back on clusters of rubs I find right near a food source and instead search for a line of rubs. I'll then follow this line—which is an obvious preferred buck travel route—some distance away from the food source before selecting and preparing a stand site.

There are a couple of important facts regarding early season rubs that hunters should know about. To begin with, antler rubs usually appear only in those places where bucks feel safe and secure letting down their guard for a brief time. Second, whitetail bucks display a real propensity for rubbing in the same general areas year after year. What this means is that, provided you continue to apply a cautious approach, it's entirely possible that you could realize an impressive string of early season bowhunting successes.

While it's an effective tactic for immature bucks, waiting in ambush near clusters of "perimeter rubs" is rarely a productive strategy for real wall-hangers. (Photo courtesy of Bob McNally.)

THE DRAWBACKS

Like all potentially productive big buck hunting tactics, there are certain negatives associated with setting up along early rub lines. Perhaps most notable of these is the fact that the tactic is a hit-and-miss proposition at best. The naturally reclusive behavior and restrictive travel patterns mature bucks often display at this time of year are most responsible for disturbingly low success rates. But there's another reason why bucks often show an obvious aversion to traveling along some of their initially established rub lines. And that reason has to do with your presence.

It's true that whitetail bucks can become somewhat preoccupied with rubbing during the early season. They might even do a bit of scraping at this time. However, they aren't doing these things to a degree where it could be considered a major distraction. Big bucks will still have nearly 100 percent of their survival instincts tuned to their surroundings. There's darn little that will escape detection by bucks under such conditions.

Another negative associated with using early rubs as a hunting aid has to do with the thickness of underbrush and foliage at this time of year. Simply put, early rubs can be darn hard to spot. Because visibility is so restricted, it's entirely possible that you could walk within just a few feet of a fresh rub and not see it. These same thick conditions can also make it extremely difficult to ascertain if a rub you've found was made at random or part of a line of rubs.

For these reasons—and many others—trying to ambush a mature whitetail buck during the early part of the archery season will remain an extremely tough chore. Notice that I used the word "tough" and not "impossible." This is because whitetail bucks will never abandon their habit of making antler rubs. Early season bowhunters would be well advised to learn how to use this very predictable aspect of big buck behavior to their advantage.

14

A SHAM IN THE DEER WOODS

by Gary Clancy

Some brand-new twists on a tried-and-true tactic are proving deadly on the smartest whitetails.

Confession time. I'm a little old-fashioned. I still hunt upland birds with a Model 12 Winchester 20-gauge that is older than I am, and I hunt waterfowl with its mate in 12-gauge. And when I take that 12-gauge and head out for a day on the marsh I'll be hunting over the same spread of mallard decoys I purchased from the old Herter's store in Waseca, Minnesota, while I was still in high school back in the '60s.

I've done a little better at "modernizing" when it comes to bowhunting, though. I've been shooting compounds for a few years now, even put sights on the last few and switched to a release. But my broadhead through all of this has remained the same. I guess you might say that I'm the kind of guy who, when he finds something that works, tends to stick with it. Take fake scrapes for instance.

I didn't dream them up. Don't know who did. But when I first read about mock scrapes probably fifteen or more years ago, the concept intrigued me, so I tried them. Like most things, they didn't work right away, but they didn't seem to scare any critters off either, so I kept on trying them. One morning, shortly before the sun rose a nice eight-point came strolling through the timber headed right for the twisted oak in which I was perched. The buck seemed to be headed somewhere important. He did not stop to look around and sniff the wind currents like his kind usually do. I figured he was late getting to his bedding area and knew it, but that was not the case. That buck marched right up to a mock scrape I had made a couple of days earlier under the overhanging branches of a maple sapling barely fifteen steps from the base of my tree. The buck never paid a bit of attention to the scrape itself, but went right to work on the overhanging branch, hooking it with his modest, white antlers, then nuzzling and nipping at the twigs. I took great pains to shift my body ever so slightly and then drew in one slow, smooth motion, but all of my worries about the buck spotting me in the tree were unfounded. I know now that the buck was so entranced by the smell and taste of that overhanging branch that I could have shaken the arrow off my rest a couple more times and he probably still would not have noticed me.

I got the buck, but just barely. My arrow sliced through him high—high enough to miss the lungs. Luckily I caught one of the major arteries and he bled to death in about six seconds, tipping over within sight of my stand and putting an end to the whipping I was already administering to myself for getting so shaken up and jerking the shot. That buck was the first I ever took over a fake scrape, but he wasn't the last and, God willing, I've got a few more left in me.

Apply a gel, paste, or liquid scent as you work up the soil in the scrape.

Some new bowhunters have probably never even heard of a mock scrape and a lot of old-timers have either given up on fake scrapes or forgotten about them, but not me. Like I said, I'm not much on changing something that works.

COMMUNICATION CENTERS

Fake scrapes work because they serve as communication centers for the bucks in the area.

Scrapes have long been thought of primarily as places where does can leave a sexy message for bucks, which they sometimes do, but just as importantly, and probably of more importance to hunters, scrapes also serve as message boards for bucks. Each buck has his own distinct odor. I guess you might compare it to our fingerprints—no two are alike. When a buck visits a mock scrape he may or may not urinate in the scrape, which is one way of leaving odor behind, but I'm convinced that the overhanging branch at the fake scrape is a far more important communication link between bucks in the neighborhood. Compare it to the message board at a big conference.

Just as everyone at that conference will stop by the message board once or twice each day of the conference to check for messages, once a buck finds a mock scrape, he will get into the habit of checking for messages. Sometimes, that can be a deadly habit.

BEAT THE RUSH

After talking with hundreds of hunters at seminars and in deer camps about mock scrapes, I'm convinced that the biggest reason many hunters experience little or no success with fake scrapes is poor timing. There is only about a three-week period each fall when mock scrapes are effective, and only one week out of those three is really hot. The mistake I see most hunters making is that they hunt over mock scrapes *after* bucks have begun pawing out their own serious breeding scrapes. By then, the prime period for hunting over fake scrapes has passed.

Dominant bucks make the first serious scrapes. I'm not talking about those pitiful little pawings you find along the edges of alfalfa fields, I'm talking churned up, serious, stinking breeding scrapes. The lesser bucks, if they do any scraping at all, will start well after the big boy has laid out a string or two. Fake scrapes really get the attention of the boss buck when you beat him to the punch. Make your fake scrapes before he makes the real thing and you stand an excellent chance of arousing the buck's curiosity to the point where he will visit your fake scrapes often in an attempt to catch the intruder bold enough to leave a mark on his turf.

I'll use fake scrapes as early as three weeks prior to the time I expect to find the first breeding scrapes. I've had bucks visit the fake scrapes within shooting hours during the first couple of weeks,

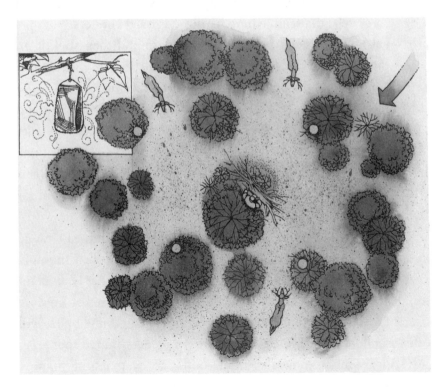

Don't skimp on the scents in your mock-scrape setup. It's a good idea to place scent bombs around your stand in order to funnel bucks to your scrapes.

but the last week is far and away the best time to be perched over a mock scrape or string of fake scrapes.

The exact dates will vary according to what part of the country you are hunting, but for our purposes, let's assume that serious scraping activity begins on November 1. That means that I will begin laying down my fake scrapes around October 10. I can expect my best action over fake scrapes during the last week of October.

TO MAKE A FAKE

Always make your fake scrapes where they are most likely to be noticed by passing deer. I'm personally not fond of field edges, because these scrapes are less likely to be visited during shooting hours. Instead, I like to make fake scrapes just off deer trails in natural woodland openings, on old logging trails, semi-open hardwood ridges, or maybe the seam where hardwoods meet conifers.

Wal-Mart does not purchase a billboard and then stick it on some dusty, country road; instead, they want that billboard in a prominent location where you and I can't miss seeing it as we cruise down the busy highway. Keep that comparison in mind when you are deciding where to place your mock scrapes. To make my fake scrapes even easier to spot I often add a fake rub or two. Once a buck has spotted the scrape his nose takes over, and from then on his visits will not hinge on being attracted visually to the fake scrape, but for that initial contact the buck often needs to see the scrape.

To be most effective, a fake scrape should be within easy range and upwind of your stand. Make sure that you have a clear shooting lane to the fake scrape. I like to position my stand so that I can comfortably take the shot while seated. One of the bonuses of hunting over a fake scrape is that you'll see more bucks, and these bucks will offer excellent opportunities for a shot at a predetermined spot.

Always make your fake scrape under an overhanging branch. Four to five feet is perfect and live branches work better than dead.

Wear rubber gloves and rubber boots so that you leave as little human scent as possible while making the fake scrape. Use a stout stick to clear the leaves and litter from an oval-shaped patch about the size of a laundry basket. Add a gel, paste, or liquid scent to the dirt and stir it in with the stick. I often use both doe-in-heat scent and a buck lure such as tarsal gland scent. Here is a dirty little trick that will keep those bucks coming back to your fake scrape again and again. Take an empty, clean 35mm film canister or baby food jar, and add a glob of paste or gel scent or take a cotton ball and saturate it with liquid scent and put it in the container. Poke holes in the lid of the container and bury it just under the surface in the mock scrape. Enough odor will escape from the container to keep those bucks coming back for more even in your absence.

You need the scrape itself to help attract the bucks, but the overhanging branch is the main communication center. In fact, most of the bucks I've had visit a fake scrape have not paid much attention to the scrape itself. When a buck works an overhanging branch he will rub his face and antlers on the branch, leaving scent from both his forehead and preorbital glands in the process. A buck, like most animals, spends a lot of time licking his own body, so when he licks and nibbles at the overhanging branch, he is leaving not only his saliva, which may be a significant odor in the world of whitetail communication, but also the scent from his urine and tarsal glands. I've seen bucks that seem to go into a trance when rubbing, licking, and nuzzling an overhanging branch. I like to place some scent on the branch itself and then add more scent by using a scent wick attached to the branch.

It has been my experience that the type of scent you use on the overhanging branch is not very important to the deer. For years I used doe-in-heat scent with fine results. Today I usually use a buck lure that incorporates forehead gland scent. Frequently I will use one type or brand of scent on the branch itself and a different one on

Keep in mind that a licking branch is an integral part of mock scraping. If there is no branch in the location of your scrape, attach your own. Always wear rubber gloves when working the mock scrape. Another neat trick of the trade is to bury a good scent dispenser directly in your scrape. A jar loaded with fresh scent will dispense odors regularly and keep bucks coming back to the location.

the scent wick. I've used the 24-Hour Scent Post from Wellington's at many of my fake scrape sites and had good results with this product. Basically, the Scent Post is a vial filled with liquid scent featuring a roller ball in the end of the bottle, much like the roller ball in some underarm deodorant bottles. The more deer work the bottle, the more scent is dispersed. The bottle is not refillable, but a single bottle will last an entire season over a fake scrape.

Fake scrapes won't work any miracles. They are not cure-alls when it comes to seeing and killing more bucks. But they are a very effective tool you can use to encourage bucks to make repeated visits to a specific location. That alone is reason enough to employ fake scrapes as far as I'm concerned, but for the hunter, the best is yet to come. When a buck does make a visit to a fake scrape you are hunting over, his attention will be riveted on that scrape, or more commonly, the overhanging branch. This makes it easy to draw without the buck detecting you. Wait for the perfect angle, pick a spot, and release. Welcome to the exciting world of hunting over fake scrapes.

15

HOT SIGN IN MIDSEASON

by Greg Miller

Hunting rub lines has long been a great early-season strategy, but finding a hot rub later on may be the best big-buck clue of all.

The antler rub I was looking at was fresh—real fresh. Shredded bark from the forearm-sized willow lay atop the two inches of snow that had fallen just twelve hours earlier. I straightened up, scanned the woods ahead, and immediately spotted another fresh rub . . . and just beyond that, another one. My pulse rate accelerated at the sight.

I had good reason to be excited about my discovery. To begin with, the fresh rubs were proof positive that the big buck I was after had survived the recently completed gun season. But just as importantly, the rubs were a rock solid indicator that the trophy whitetail obviously felt at ease traveling through this spot. Now it was merely a matter of finding a stand site that would allow me to take advantage of this knowledge.

WHAT LATE RUBS TELL US

Most deer hunters are aware of the significance that antler rubs play in the lives of whitetail bucks during the early season and pre-rut periods. In a nutshell, bucks make lines of rubs along the travel routes they use when traveling back and forth between bedding and feeding areas. Most hunters also know that lines showing the greatest number of large rubs likely are the preferred travel routes of the more mature bucks in a given area.

What many hunters aren't aware of, however, is that they can also use rubs to key in on bucks later in the season. To me, finding fresh and/or "reworked" rubs at this time of year is a clear signal from the buck responsible for those rubs. That signal means the buck is back and it's time to once again put the hunt on him — right now.

But bucks actually have a somewhat different reason for becoming "rub-active" late in the season. Simply put, late rubs are a big buck's way of announcing to all other bucks that he has returned from his rutting travels and has once again taken up residence in his core area.

Along with making and re-freshening a certain number of sign-post rubs throughout their core areas, bucks also will make and re-freshen rubs along a select few of their more preferred late-season travel routes. It's these rubs that I feel are most important to hunters.

My good friend and fellow big buck hunter, Stan Potts, agrees. "Basically, late rubs are just a spin-off of early rubs," he states. "By that I mean you'll usually find them in the same places where you find early rubs."

But Potts quickly added that there's one very important difference between early pre-rut rubs and late rubs. "It sometimes can be

Rub-line hunting used to be thought of as only an early-season tactic; however, bucks returning to their old pre-rut haunts late in the season will also rub. Look for fresh sign along their old travel routes and near food sources.

tough to determine which of their rub lines big bucks are using most often during the pre-rut. Their travel routines could be dictated by the location of food, water, antlerless deer, or maybe even other factors. That's not the case later on in the season, however. At this time of year the travel patterns of mature bucks are going to be dictated by only one thing. And that one thing is the location of a particular preferred food. Here in Illinois, where I live, I know that late-season whitetails are going to be hammering the nearest standing and picked cornfields."

WHEN TO HUNT LATE RUBS

One aspect of late rub activity I've found quite beneficial concerns using fresh rubs to determine a buck's direction of travel. This is so critical that I almost always restrict my late-season hunting efforts to the early evening hours. Obviously, it's imperative I locate those routes that targeted bucks are using when they travel from their bedding areas to feeding areas.

I'm sure some hunters are wondering why I hunt late season bucks only during the evenings. The reason is simple. Try as I might, I have yet to find a way that allows me to get to my morning stand sites without alerting at least a few (and most times a lot) of deer.

For those of you who think that spooking a few deer in the morning is no big deal, think again. Keep in mind that we're talking about the late season here. The cumulative effects of months of hunting pressure will have taken their toll on mature bucks. They simply aren't going to put up with much in the way of human intrusion.

Potts told me that he also prefers to hunt only evenings during the late season. "I'm in the same boat as a lot of hunters in that my late-season hunting areas are literally overrun with antlerless deer," he stated. "Sure, I might be able to get to my morning stand without bumping the big bucks I'm hunting. But it's virtually impossible to go anywhere on my property in the morning without spooking a bunch of does, fawns, and small bucks."

Like me, Potts pays attention only to rub lines where the rubs face away from the food source. These types of rub lines indicate evening travel routes, and almost always link bedding areas with feeding areas. And remember that there's no such thing as a "set distance" between these two places.

BE CAREFUL

There's another very important factor hunters must keep in mind when hunting near late rubs. This factor has to do with stand site selection. As Potts put it, "Late-season hunters quickly find out that the woods look a lot different now than they did earlier in the season. A lot of the underbrush has died off and all the trees will have lost their leaves.

"What this means is that the woods are a lot more open now. Mature bucks realize this and, as a result, rely on their eyes a lot more than normal to warn them of potentially dangerous situations. And trust me, they don't miss much either."

This is without a doubt the biggest downfall of setting up close to late rubs. Hey folks, rubs are where they are because the bucks that made them feel secure traveling through those spots. And the reason they feel secure is because they're confident they'll be able to detect potentially dangerous situations long before the situations become life threatening.

Because of this, Potts urges hunters to take some extra time when selecting and preparing late-season stand sites. "I have two basic guidelines I adhere to when I'm putting up portable treestands during the late-season," he told me. "The first is that my stands are placed to take full advantage of existing wind conditions. And second, I'm going to look for trees that offer me at least some natural cover. I like to use clusters of large branches and trees with split trunks to help break up my outline as much as possible. Even then, I still occasionally get picked off by big bucks."

I well remember an experience I had with a big buck during a past late-season hunt. My stand was nestled nearly thirty feet from

No other type of deer sign can tell hunters as much about the habits and patterns of mature bucks as antler rubs. This hunter was on stand 20 yards from a rub line.

the ground among a jumble of thigh-sized branches in a huge oak. A red-hot rub line ran by just twenty yards from the base of the oak.

The sun had just slipped below the horizon on that cold December day when I heard a deer approaching. It wasn't long before I spotted a long-tined ten-pointer seventy-five yards out, slowly working towards me along the rub line. A slight breeze was blowing directly from the buck to me, so I was confident it was a done deal.

The buck was still better than thirty yards away when he suddenly slammed on the brakes. I instinctively tucked my chin into my chest and closed my eyes. I kept my eyes squeezed shut for nearly a half-minute before sneaking a peek. It was a mistake. The big deer was looking directly up into my eyes.

The results were both predictable and devastating. The ten-pointer let out a loud snort, spun on his hind legs, and went crashing off. I never saw him again during that late season.

This experience perfectly illustrates just how sharp mature whitetails can be during the late season. Initially, I was under the impression that the big deer simply sensed my presence. But over time I became more convinced that, even though I'd taken great pains to keep it from happening, something about my setup had caught the buck's attention.

UNDERSTANDING DIFFERENT TYPES OF LATE RUBS

As mentioned previously, whitetail bucks seem to use late rubs as both communication signposts and as a way of monitoring deer activity along their travel routes. I've taken advantage of both types of rub situations over the years.

For instance, the fresh, late-season rub line mentioned at the beginning of this chapter led me to my best ever muzzleloader buck. A bit of additional scouting of the rub line showed that the big deer was traveling to a nearby picked cornfield to feed. Since the area was relatively undisturbed, I opted to spend the early evening hours on a stand situated near the edge of the field.

My first two sittings confirmed that the cornfield was the primary feeding spot for the majority of the deer on the property. I counted more than two dozen antlerless animals and a half-dozen immature bucks during my first sit. The numbers were even higher on my second hunt.

The big buck finally made his appearance on the third afternoon. I was absorbed in watching a couple good-looking 2½-year-old bucks when I happened to notice movement near the top of a hill 150 yards straight out in front of me. The next thing I knew a huge buck was standing atop the hill.

Though the buck was well within range of the .50-caliber Thompson/Center Encore I was carrying, I was forced to wait. Several antlerless deer were feeding close around the giant whitetail. I simply wouldn't risk taking a shot until the buck was in the clear.

The next five minutes dragged by agonizingly slow. But in the end things actually worked out for the better. The buck had cut the distance by a good twenty yards when the time finally came to take the shot. I anchored the monster nine-pointer on the spot.

I've used signpost rubs to take several late-season trophies, but one in particular stands out most in my mind. The hunt involved a giant non-typical that I'd been chasing for nearly two full seasons.

I'd hunted the big deer to the point of exhaustion during the early archery season. But all I had to show for my efforts was a very sore back and a somewhat frustrated outlook on the late season. Then I got a huge break.

My brother, Jeff, was doing some routine scouting on our property when he happened to find a half-dozen steaming fresh rubs on six- to eight-inch poplar trees. The poplars were located near one corner of a snow-covered alfalfa field that the local deer herd was using as a main food source. Luckily, I'd placed a portable stand earlier in the season in a big gnarly oak that stood just twenty yards from the rubs.

I'll do away with any suspense by telling you that I arrowed the monster eighteen-pointer the very first afternoon that I sat on the stand in the oak. In essence, the trophy whitetail had been greatly responsible for his own demise. The rubs he'd made on the poplars told me that the buck was definitely back in the area and exactly where he felt the safest when walking out to feed on the alfalfa.

Stan Potts told me he recently used a cluster of fresh rubs to figure out an ambush for a big buck during his home state's late archery season. "I was scouting a chunk of timber that bordered a small standing cornfield when I found the rubs," he said. "At that point I was able to eliminate several other likely looking spots I'd found earlier. I was able to do this because there were no fresh rubs in those other spots. As it turned out, I ended up shooting a 150-class, ten-pointer the first time I hunted near the rubs."

BE READY FOR ANYTHING

There is one similarity between early rubs and late rubs that is well worth mentioning. As with the pre-rut period, it's not unusual at all for a number of different bucks to be using the same signpost rubs and/or rub lines in the late season. In fact, if conditions are right, it's not unusual for several mature bucks to be relating to the same late rubs.

During a late-season muzzleloader hunt in western Iowa a couple years back I watched eleven different bucks work the same rub. Three of the bucks were what I would consider solid "shooters." Unfortunately, none of those three deer came within range.

The most obvious benefit of using late antler rubs as scouting and hunting aids is the fact that they're so visible. Because of this, I'm usually able to effectively scout my late-season hunting areas without creating too much of a disturbance. And that's a big plus.

Along those lines, there's one last thing I'd like to discuss. The most common mistake made by late-season hunters is that they try to get too close too soon. In other words, they do way too much stomping around when looking for and trying to figure out rubs and rub lines. They do the same thing when searching for late-season stand sites.

My philosophy on the subject is simple. I like to start out by setting up in spots where my intrusions might cause only a minor disturbance. I then use data collected (mostly through observation) during my hunts to figure out if—and exactly where—I need to relocate my stands.

Twenty-plus years of study on the subject have taught me that no other type of deer sign can tell hunters nearly as much about the habits and patterns of mature bucks as antler rubs. This "rule" applies regardless of whether you're talking about pre-rut or late-season whitetails. As long as bucks are wearing headgear, they're going to leave constant reminders of their daily activities.

16

FOLLOW YOUR DOES

by Dave Justmann

Successful buck hunters learn to read the rut's current stage
by watching the does.

Even though hunters normally think about the rut in terms of buck activity, it's really the does that call the shots. Overall, does within a given area come into heat at about the same time every year. However, the exact date for each doe varies. Rutting activity on any particular property is dictated by the heat dates of the does that frequent that property and by how much bucks harass them. Watch the does, and you'll learn how, when, and where to cross paths with the bucks.

THE UNEASINESS BEGINS

A small percentage of does come into heat about a month before the peak of the rut. This, combined with the bucks' rising hormone levels, causes the bucks to start cruising for hot does from early evening through early morning. They scent-check all the other deer they encounter, either up close or from a distance. Many times a buck will aggressively run up to a doe to smell her. Because the vast majority of does are not yet ready to breed, they run off. This scenario happens day after day, which explains why does are often nervous and alert during this period. They're constantly looking in all directions and listening for the unwelcome approach of a harassing buck. So when does seem unduly nervous at the sudden sight or sound of other deer, that's a good indication that the pre-rut has begun.

During this period bucks primarily follow established deer trails as they search for does, making them vulnerable to straightforward trail watching. After a couple weeks of searching they will have created rub lines and scrape lines along the routes they frequent. These are prime trails along which to intercept them.

Hunter's Specialties pro-staff member Pat Reeve has guided numerous hunters to mature bucks during this period, a time when he finds it easiest to pattern and harvest bigger bucks. He emphasizes that re-scouting a hunting area now keeps his finger on the pulse of what's happening in his area. During his scouting, Reeve exercises extreme caution not to leave human scent behind. He wears rubber boots and gloves, avoids touching brush, and stays downwind of bedding areas.

He feels that hunting during the two weeks immediately preceding the pre-rut is a mistake. During hours on stand, a hunter's scent wafts into the woods, and deer spot him entering and leaving in the dark. The deer realize they are being hunted and will remain nocturnal through the pre-rut. By contrast, if hunters in low-pressure

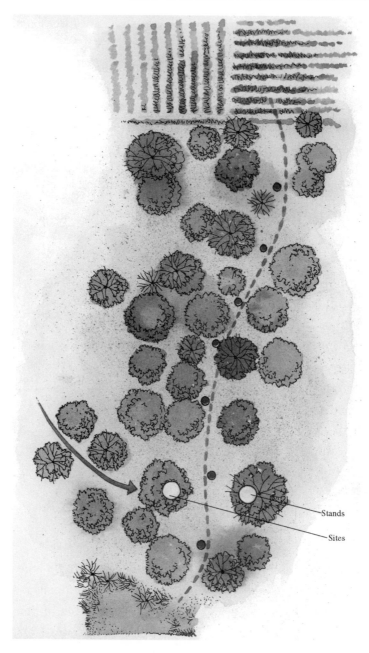

Drag-rag scent lines are an excellent way to attract bucks to your stand during the rut. Here's a typical scent-drag setup used by the pros.

areas wait until the pre-rut, they will often find undisturbed deer that travel during shooting hours.

A couple of seasons ago, Reeve arrived at his hunting area during the pre-rut to re-scout. He found a heavily used scrape line on a bluffside bench where he knew does frequently bedded after feeding overnight in the farm fields below. He quickly hung a stand and left the area before the deer began their evening movement.

The next morning he parked on the backside of the steep bluff, hiked up and over the top, and then dropped down the stand side of the ridge while pulling a scent-soaked drag rag behind him. About 8 A.M. Pat spotted a couple of does working their way up from the bottom. A 130-class buck spotted the does, closed the gap to scent-check them, and then veered off. The does continued up the bluff. After milling around a while, they decided they were safe from the buck and bedded down within sight of Reeve.

An hour later the same buck appeared on a cross-hill trail about fifty yards above Reeve. After every fifth or sixth step, the buck would drop his head and sniff the ground. When the buck hit the drag line, he immediately turned and followed it like he was on a string. At twenty-five yards, Reeve took him through both lungs with a Muzzy-tipped arrow. The hunter watched the buck lie down for good just fifty yards away. The does had been the key to luring the buck into the area, and Reeve's expertise had done the rest.

NO DOES

During the last few days before the rut shifts into high gear, expect a sudden, marked decline in doe sightings. The bucks roam all day long at this time, but the antlerless deer are tired of being harassed, especially in areas with high buck-to-doe ratios. Now the does bed close to food and move only as far as necessary. As soon as they're done feeding, they bed down again to hide.

LONESOME FAWNS AND GIDDY DOES

Repeated sightings of fawns traveling without their mothers are a good indicator that the main rut has arrived. Just before coming into heat, a doe either drives her fawns away or runs until they are too tired to keep up. Lone fawn sightings tell you that you're within the home range of a doe in heat.

Travel funnels that also afford a good view and listening post for the surrounding ridges and openings are ideal stand sites. Listen for the ruckus of brush breaking as bucks chase does. Similarly, listen for frequent grunts from a buck that is traveling through the woods at a fast pace. He's likely on the trail of a hot doe. If you see or hear a doe being chased by a buck, don't hesitate to rush over there. Deer loop repeatedly during the chase and may come past you within range.

Even if you merely observe a doe acting giddy and holding her tail in an unnatural position, beat over to cover the route she just followed. She is likely in heat, and bucks will pick up her scent trail. It's common for every buck in the vicinity to come by within the first half-hour. Even if you don't happen to see the doe, you may still spot one of the pursuing bucks. A buck that is trotting through the woods with his nose just a foot above ground that never stops to look for danger is on a hot doe's scent trail. More bucks may well be on the way.

Trophy whitetail outfitter John Hambleton has observed that when a doe comes into heat in his area, which has a high buck-to-doe ratio, a buck will often herd her away from the larger woodlots and into small groves or isolated patches of tall grass. Here they escape the harassment and constant challenges of other bucks.

One of Hambleton's favorite strategies during this period is to sit beside a fenceline on a compact portable stool that assembles in just a few seconds. Here he intercepts bucks leaving the main woods to check the remote islands of cover for bedded mating pairs.

FAWNS REUNITED WITH THEIR MOTHERS

After a doe is bred, she'll reunite with her fawns. The family unit's movements will then be limited during the post-rut period to avoid continued harassment by bucks. According to outfitter Tom Indrebo, buck sign means very little now. The bucks are searching far and wide, and they no longer regularly visit rub or scrape lines. Hunters afield now are tempted to leave their stands early. This is the most difficult period of the rut in which to maintain confidence in a stand, even though it's an even better time to connect with a buck than during the peak of breeding activity. Sure, a hunter won't see as many deer, but when one does come by, the chance of it being a buck is quite high.

One time Indrebo positioned two hunting buddies a couple hundred yards apart on a ridge that had held lots of does throughout the fall. Consequently, the bucks had been cruising it relentlessly. One of the hunters spotted a huge buck passing by out of range during midmorning and watched the buck bed. Around 3 P.M. a doe happened by. The buck spotted her, immediately jumped to his feet, and began his pursuit. The unreceptive doe came running past the hunter, with the 160-class buck close beyond. Seconds later, Indrebo's client brought the trophy down with a well-placed slug.

RESUMPTION OF NORMALITY

Normal doe activity resumes after the bucks tire of constantly coming up empty-handed. Both the does and bucks feed longer each day during this post-rut period. The bucks, especially, are tired and run down. Their metabolisms tell them it's time to forget the mating foolishness and feed heavily to prepare for winter. Putting out a nutritional supplement now, such as Cutting Edge Sustain, does more than just attract bucks to your hunting property. It provides them with the protein, vitamins, and minerals they'll need to fully recover before the rigors of winter.

Stay out of your hunting area until the pre-rut. Then quietly scout for rubs and scrapes, keeping the wind in your favor.

Your hunting strategy now should be the same as it was before the rut began. Hunt bedding areas in the morning and field edges in the evening.

GIDDY FAWNS

After the main rut has passed, most hunters think that breeding activity has ended. However, any does that failed to conceive on the first go 'round will come back into heat a month later. Some doe fawns also will come into heat now, when they are about six months old. Giddy fawn behavior now indicates that the second rut has arrived. Even the buck fawns act differently, with a small percentage of them getting in on the breeding, especially in areas with low buck-to-doe ratios.

To cash in on this second rut, a hunter is well served by going to the part of his state with the best food and the least severe post-rut weather. For example, a study in Wisconsin revealed that forty percent of the doe fawns in the rich farmland of the state's southern counties are bred when less than a year old. By contrast, the number was only a few percent in the big-woods counties to the north. And in Nebraska, research indicates that about sixty percent of doe fawns get bred.

In the face of the rapidly approaching winter, bucks are focused on feeding, not breeding. They won't be searching out the hot does. They'll simply detect a hot doe during their routine activities. Then they'll stay with that doe for the next few days, breeding her as long as she remains receptive. To hunt bucks during the second rut, key in on the few remaining choice feeding areas. Hot does that show up to feed will have bucks in tow.

Throughout the stages of the rut, watch the does in your specific hunting area for clues. The bucks simply respond to doe activity. Learning from doe sightings will help a hunter recognize the best times and places to intercept the does' potential suitors.

HUNT THE RIGHT SCRAPES

After the summertime bachelor herds disband, each buck picks a core area where he will frequently bed from now until the main rut. He will venture out of that area in the evening to feed. He'll make small scrapes along the edges of his feeding area, but won't revisit them. These scrapes tell a hunter where a buck feeds after dark, but they won't help him pinpoint where the buck will be during the day.

A few weeks before the rut's peak, scrapes take on new meaning, with bucks regularly freshening the best ones. In any given area, bucks will have one or two particular species of trees that they prefer to scrape beneath. The denser the cover around a scrape, the more likely the buck will be to visit it during shooting hours.

The best scrapes to hunt are unusually large and deep and located beneath a low-hanging, nibbled branch. The scrape depth, amount of branch damage, and number of nearby scrapes and rubs all indicate the level of visitation. Often, the best scrapes are located in the mustiest soil within the buck's core area. The dampness and organic matter in the soil hold the scent of deer urine better than dry or sandy soil.

One hunter I know takes matters into his own hands. He hunts a property that has only sandy soil on it. To make matters worse, the browse line is so high that the deer can't nibble any branches of their preferred tree species, oak. Consequently, he'd never found any regularly visited scrapes on this property. One year he decided to make his own ideal scrape site beside one of his treestands, located between two ultra-dense bedding areas. He tossed a rope over one of the oak branches, pulled it down until the tips were three feet from the ground, and tied the rope to the tree's trunk. Then he dug a hole beneath this branch and filled it back up with ideal soil from another property. The deer took the cue and starting scraping there almost immediately.

17

SCENT STRATEGIES FOR THE RUT

by Jeff Murray

In order to propagate the species, bucks must locate breeding partners efficiently during a very narrow window of time (does go in and out of estrus within thirty-six to forty-eight hours). So if you can get your hands on a hot estrus scent, here are the best methods of using it to lure bucks within bow or gun range.

SCENTS FOR THE STANDING SHOT

It sounds silly, but many hunters mistakenly hunt the wrong places and then wonder why their deer scents failed to produce. The real key to luring bucks is setting up where they are most likely to aggressively pursue does during daylight hours. This is a huge topic, but suffice it to say that you better hole up in or near doe bedding thickets; the open stuff, no matter how loaded it is with sign, just won't do. And since effective rut hunting invariably revolves around dense vegetation, *positioning* bucks becomes a top priority. Nothing is more frustrating during the rut than helplessly watching a suicidal, stiff-legged buck slip around you without being able to get off a quality shot.

The solution, of course, is the judicious application of deer scent to stop that hot-to-trot buck precisely where you want him. You can also use scent to angle a wayward buck your way so he doesn't take the wrong fork in the trail. Both objectives are best accomplished with a simple technique: Use a tree branch or dead stick to lay down scent where you want the buck's nose to stop. For heavy cover, you'll need to factor in the distance between the tip of his nose and the kill zone. For instance, if you're dealing with a two-foot-wide shooting lane, you better place some scent a good foot ahead of the opening. Now, when the buck's nose comes in contact with the scent, he'll offer an unobstructed view of his vitals.

The above formula is predicated on a pair of critical assumptions. One is that you aren't applying too much scent. Although scents vary in quality and potency, dozens of close encounters have taught me that less is always better than more. Two drops—one on the ground, another two feet up on a bush, stump, or rock—is plenty. Using more is asking for trouble. The penalty for overindulgence is stiff: unpredictable behavior. The buck may stop dead a few feet short. Or he may veer suddenly and circle without presenting a quality shot. Still another scenario involves a badly spooked buck—or a spooked doe preceding the buck—hoofing it out of the area. Simply stated, fresh urine products work best when applied sparingly.

Another critical element is not polluting the immediate area with your scent. Impeccable personal hygiene is a good start, but you still can't take any chances. Once again, apply scent with a stick—as long as eight feet to reach around obstructions or over tall

The judicious use of deer scents in the center of a shooting lane can help stop a buck for a perfect shot opportunity.

grass—to avoid touching the spot where you want the deer to stop. Incidentally, you can apply scent directly to the tip of the stick or saturate a clean rag, securing it at the tip with a rubber binder.

FAKE-BELIEVE TRAILS

A traditional method of luring rutting bucks to gun or bow is laying down a scent trail. Once again, it's possible to screw things up by glossing over subtle-but-important details. Naturally, a contaminated deer trail is counterproductive (the buck interprets this message as a hunter following a buck!), so work carefully with the rag/stick combo.

And by all means don't make the mistake of letting bucks track your mock-trail backwards. If you fail to reapply scent along the way, your trail grows weaker with distance. Since investigating bucks pursue a trail toward a stronger scent source, not toward a weaker one, you may never see this buck near your treestand or ground blind.

To entice big bucks like this one, it's important to lay scent trails strategically. Haphazard deployment will just tip off deer to your presence.

THE FIGURE-EIGHT

Suppose you've located a hot funnel where bucks squeeze through on a fairly regular basis. You won't have to mess with fake-believe trails because you know a buck's going to head your way sooner or later. The only question is . . . where exactly? Bowhunters are especially vulnerable to the "close but not close enough" encounter with a rutting buck, and here's a maneuver that's sure to put Mr. Hat Rack in your lap.

Lay out a scent trail that looks like the infinity symbol (shaped like an elongated figure-eight on its side), and place your stand at the intersection of the two circles. Virtually every buck hitting your scent trail will end up right on top of you. You may want to practice this ploy in a field or parking lot so you can pull it off in the pre-dawn darkness. You can use the stick approach, alluded to above, but a simple "drag rag" tied to your boots is adequate because you won't have to reapply scent—no matter which route the buck takes on the scent trail, he's going to end up at the intersection of the two loops in front of your stand.

You can't expect bucks to zero in on deer scent like vultures on road kill, but these time-tested strategies will definitely up the ante when the rut puts bucks on the prowl.

18

SECOND-RUT REALITY

by Bill Winke

Two ruts are better than one. But is there really a second rut? And if there is, what's the best way to hunt it?

I remember doing an interview with Myles Keller once nearly a decade ago, and it really bugged me when we were finished. I wanted his assessment of the opportunities being discussed to match my own so that I could feel better about what I was doing, but it didn't work out that way. Most of Myles's trophies were being taken well after the part of the season when I was shooting my deer. It wouldn't have been so bad but Myles's bucks, as a class, were bigger than the ones I was shooting. It got me to wondering what this guy knew that I didn't. Since then I've spent a lot more time hunting the late sea-

Although less intense than the primary rut, the secondary rut can produce extraordinary action late in the season. Look for bucks wind-checking food sources for hot does.

son and two years ago I was rewarded when I shot my biggest buck to date at the end of December.

The late season—second rut or no second rut—has a consistency to it that the rut lacks. The rut is random; the buck you've been scouting all summer and early fall may be five miles away during the rut. There aren't many really big bucks anywhere and when you focus on shooting only fully mature bucks you have cut the field by about ninety percent. It almost becomes a game of hunting specific deer. During the rut, however, expecting a single buck to act like you want it to, or even expecting it to stay in the area you are hunting, isn't usually going to pay off.

But in the late season you have better odds of being able to focus on that one buck because he won't be roaming. You can actually pattern a buck on his food sources when the season is winding down. That doesn't mean he's going to be easy—he'll be one of the spookiest bucks you'll ever hunt—but at least you'll know where he is. Like Myles Keller, a surprising number of really successful buck hunters never worry a bit if their tags are still in their pockets when the primary rut ends because they know the season is far from over.

The second rut is only one of several factors that influence late-season buck behavior. In fact, when compared to hunting pressure and weather, it ranks a distant third. When the conditions are right, however, the second rut can lead to opportunities for taking a trophy buck after most hunters have given up for the year.

HOW GOOD IS THE SECOND RUT?

When comparing the intensity of the second rut to that of the primary rut we need only to look at the numbers to get some idea of what to expect.

When the ratio of does to bucks is higher than about four or five to one (as it is in most loosely managed hunting areas), there will be some adult does that simply don't get bred during their first estrus cycle. Also, some young does don't come into their initial estrus until a time frame that would be the second cycle for most others in the herd. Any does that still haven't been bred after the primary rut will cycle into estrus again twenty-eight days later. (When trying to take advantage of the second rut, first determine the peak of the primary rut and add twenty-eight days to pinpoint the most likely peak of any secondary breeding.)

Additionally, in nutrition-rich ranges, such as most parts of the upper Midwest and portions of the Northeast, as many as eighty percent of all doe fawns will be bred during their first autumn. (On poorer ranges, typified by a lack of agricultural crops, the rate is still twenty-five percent or more.) These doe fawns usually come into their very first estrus at least one cycle later than their mothers—again making them prime candidates for the second rut.

When you consider that the average adult doe has 1.5 fawns on these quality ranges, and that half will be does, the numbers suggest there will be at least sixty percent as many does in estrus during the second rut as during the first. This would lead one to believe that the second rut has sixty percent of the overall intensity of the first, but unfortunately it doesn't.

The primary rut has already taken the edge off the breeding excitement of the younger bucks, and with the gun season having come and gone in most areas, there are now fewer total bucks around. This results in less intensity and less competition. Also, the hunting pressure has made the remaining bucks very shy and unlikely to move much during the day. Most second rut activity takes place at night.

So how much activity does the second rut generate? You will see a little chasing and cruising, but nothing like you saw a month earlier. On average, if you are hunting typical locations that see moderate hunting pressure you may or may not even notice. Remember, this breeding is taking place in early December in most parts of the country. That timing in itself may work for you or it may work against you.

A classic example of the timing working well was the second rut in Iowa a few years ago. November was a very warm month throughout the entire country that year and especially so in the Midwest. Things were pretty dead. There was very little daytime movement and it was likely that many does didn't get bred simply because of the logistics. At least that would explain why the second rut was so strong that year. More does than usual made it through the primary rut without being bred, spurring greater buck activity than normal when temperatures finally did cool off in early December. The owner of the property bordering the land I hunt shot a Boone & Crockett buck during the first weekend of December that year (opening weekend of the gun season), and the buck was fully engaged in chasing a doe in an open food plot when Ed shot it. That's a rare situation in which the timing of the second rut worked out to the hunter's advantage.

Now, let me paint another picture that is a bit more realistic. The late November gun season is over and the woods seem completely sterile. You don't see anything moving as you sit on your stand overlooking a bottleneck that had been a tremendous rut funnel during your bowhunts in early November. It remains dead there day after day—so much for the second rut. The only way you're going to take a nice buck in this setting is to wait until they are once again moving a little during the day. That may take a couple of weeks with no hunting pressure. Most of the serious late-season hunters I know don't even start looking for nice bucks until about two weeks after the firearms season is over. In many areas of the country this time frame is well past the second rut.

ELEMENTS AFFECTING LATE-SEASON BEHAVIOR

It's safe to say that the second rut has a smaller effect on the behavior of late season bucks than two other factors, hunting pressure and temperature.

As long as there are still-hunters in the woods bumping into deer and leaving scent, it's impossible for a wary old buck to completely relax and start moving naturally. The does also become unbelievably skittish under these conditions. Where you find heavy hunting pressure you can forget about seeing much activity during the second rut. For example, by the time of the second rut in Michigan the deer have just come through hard pressure during the regular gun season, and the late blackpowder hunters are now reminding them that it's still too early to start planning a Survivor Party. You're not going to see much chasing during the second rut in Michigan, but if you hunt an isolated ranch in Nebraska the hunting pressure in November and early December is much less and the probability that you'll see bucks chasing does during the second rut is much better.

The most reliable factor influencing late season buck movement is the weather. Whenever it gets extremely cold in December and January the deer will feed more heavily, and this will make them more vulnerable. Usually, the first bitter cold snap of the year occurs in late December, well after the second rut. If you are looking for late-season action in areas with fairly heavy hunting pressure, forget the second rut and wait until the deer have calmed back down and then focus on the feeding patterns that develop when it gets bone-chilling cold. If it never gets cold, you may never see any real daytime movement by mature bucks.

STRATEGIES FOR THE SECOND RUT

If you hunt in an area where the hunting pressure is light there is some hope you'll catch buck activity during the second rut. At this

The second rut is largely a big-buck affair. However, bucks that have been worn down by the rigors of the first rut aren't up for wide-ranging doe chases. Look for fresh sign on a big buck's home turf.

time it is best to focus entirely on the doe family groups, much like you probably did during the peak breeding phase of the primary rut a month earlier. The strategy is fairly simple: Hunt the doe bedding areas in the mornings and the doe feeding areas in the evenings. By this point in the season you should know the locations of these places pretty well.

Assuming your state doesn't have the proper timing and/or the moderate hunting pressure required to make the second rut pay off, you can still be successful during the late season by focusing on food. Any carbohydrate- or protein-rich grain crop is the first place to start. The ideal setup is an unharvested cornfield. Even harvested fields will draw deer when the deep freeze hits.

Food sources that are hidden from roads and located well away from human eyes are the most likely to produce big buck action at this time of the season. Go out of your way to locate such remote spots. Generally, gaining access to hunt an area well after opening day is not nearly as tough as it was earlier. You may even be able to spot a nice buck, or at least a group of feeding does, by slowly cruising county roads just before dark, so don't rule out that option.

After locating at least one active feeding area, don't make a move until you see a buck big enough to interest you. You'll be tempted to move in and set up a stand sooner, but if you haven't actually seen a buck you'd like to shoot, the risk of spooking the does before he shows up is too great. Be patient; watch and learn.

The last thing you want to do is barge right in and spook the deer off their feeding area before you even have a good chance to pattern the buck that's using it. Remember, these are extremely wary deer and it may take the buck a while to feel comfortable enough to use the field during daylight. With the first hint of human intrusion, he's going to be back on a nocturnal pattern faster than you can say "unfilled tag." If the buck is not alarmed and starts to show himself, he will likely continue to display more or less the same behavior for several days, at least until there is a major weather change or until he gets bumped.

Pay close attention to exactly how he enters the feeding area (usually it is just at or just after the end of legal shooting time). What trail did he use? What was the wind direction? What time was it? All of these facts are important when setting up an ambush the next evening.

Choosing a location for the ambush is a very delicate matter. Bucks won't use the same exact trail to enter their feeding areas each day. In fact, they don't always use the same feeding area each day. So, you'll have to play it conservatively. Late-season hunting is a waiting game. Make sure that you can get out of the area after shooting time expires without alarming a single deer. If you can't, you are using the wrong stand location.

Smart bucks (a good definition for all bucks that have survived the general firearms season) will often arrive last at a feeding area, following all the does and immature bucks. So even if you only spook a couple of does while heading back to your vehicle, you've made it more difficult to tag the buck on future hunts.

If you aren't completely sure of the buck's pattern, the best starting point is a stand that serves two purposes. Primarily, it should be located in a place where you can watch the entire feeding area from downwind. This way you can verify what is happening from a safe distance. Secondly, if at all possible, choose a spot that offers some hope that deer may pass within range. This way you won't spend an entire evening of precious hunting time with no chance for a shot.

What you see will tell you what to do next. As you learn the buck's patterns better, move in closer. Always keep the wind and stand entry and exit trails in the forefront of your mind when fine-tuning stand placement. Don't get too hasty, but when the opportunity presents itself, make your move.

Even though the peak of the rut has passed, there are still opportunities for taking a nice buck each season. In fact, some of the biggest bucks are taken after the primary rut. For the select few who hunt under the right circumstances, the second rut will increase the activity level of bucks around the doe groups in places where they concentrate (feeding and bedding areas). But if hunting pressure or poor timing makes the second rut an unlikely choice for you, don't give up without at least trying to pattern a buck on his food sources when hunting pressure slackens and the weather turns brutally cold.

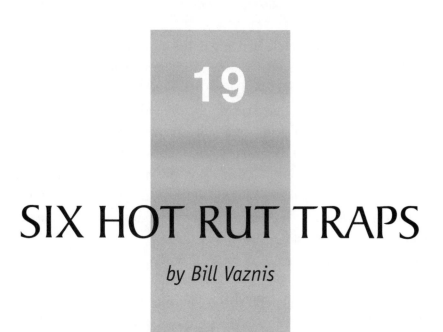

19

SIX HOT RUT TRAPS

by Bill Vaznis

*When the moon of madness is upon us, trophy bucks are suckers
for the right setup.*

The peak of the rut is the time most of us dream about all year
long. This is when we can expect to see wide-racked bucks
chasing does around pastures at first light with wild abandon or
brazenly crossing open fields at noon, seemingly oblivious to the
possibility of danger. Indeed, bucks we never knew existed suddenly
pop up out of nowhere, giving us one quick chance to score before
they disappear from our lives forever.

The problem is that many hunters fail to change tactics when
the rut begins, relying instead on old information to help them

score. No longer are bucks bedding in the same tangles every morning or feeding in the same beanfields night after night. They may not even be living on the same farm anymore. Indeed, they may be holed up with a hot doe in a nearby swamp today and then on a faraway ridge nose-to-tail with yet another estrus doe three days later.

But all is not lost. Bucks may seem unpredictable once the rut kicks into high gear, but that won't stop you from planning a lethal ambush. In fact, this is one of the best times to tag the biggest buck of your life. Here are six deadly ambush strategies guaranteed to get you a shot at your best buck ever this fall.

RIDGES

Does and fawns generally feed low and then bed high during the middle of the day. You may find bucks sniffing around the fields at first light for a doe near estrus, but once the does have left the open areas, the bucks will be up on the ridges looking for them.

Sure, you could set up a treestand on one of the trails leading up the hill and away from the field, and if a buck connects with an estrus doe at first light you might get a shot at him as he follows her toward her bedding area.

A more logical plan, however, would be to do just what a lonesome buck does to maximize his chances of hooking up with a hot doe right after first light. That is, he checks all the trails leading up the hill away from the morning food source by sneaking along a ridge that runs perpendicular to the doe trails. This way he can quickly determine if there are any eligible ladies in the immediate vicinity.

So where do you put your stand? To maximize your chances, look for those entrance and exit routes bucks prefer as they move from one woodlot to the next in search of does. A fenceline, a narrowing, the nearest piece of thick cover, and a brushy finger are all good places to look for sign. Erect your stand to cover both the route the buck will take to intersect the greatest number of doe trails in the morning and the route a buck will take to exit the woodlot as he travels to the next bedding area.

WILD APPLE ORCHARDS

Bucks love apples; ask any orchard owner in deer country. Given the opportunity, they will eat the buds, stems, and, of course, the apples—right down to the last piece of fruit under the tree, leaving the farmer very little to show for his labors.

But the apple orchards I'm talking about are wild, left to the vagaries of nature and well hidden from man. Abandoned as they seem, bucks patrol the scrubby trees looking for estrus does when the moon of madness hits, just as they would any other food source frequented by family groups of does and fawns at this time of the year.

My favorite apple orchards lie between a primary food source, such as an alfalfa lot or beanfield, and a bedding area preferred by those family groups of does and fawns. These orchards often function as transition zones and are thus hot in the morning when does are heading out to bed down and again in the evening when does are on the feed.

How can you locate abandoned orchards? That's easy. Study area topo maps for rows of green circular squiggles that indicate an orchard, usually found off the beaten track near abandoned farms. Shoe leather can later confirm your suspicions, but you don't have to hunt just orchards. A single tree can be just as productive, and these are easy to locate in the spring. Just look for ten- to fifteen-foot trees with round crowns and lots of pink and white blossoms. Given good weather conditions, those trees will bear fruit in the fall.

Over the years I have caught several bucks bedding down near apple trees or in apple orchards, presumably waiting for does to come and feed. It has happened to me so often that now when I sneak in and around apple trees, I look for bedded bucks as well as those on the move.

Positioning yourself to intercept as many does as possible is a great tactic for waylaying rutting bucks.

A few years ago I watched a buck enter an orchard and then stay put. Curious, I did some sneaking and peaking and caught the fat nine-pointer bedded down on a slight knoll above the orchard. From that vantage point he could see if any does were coming in to feed. I took him in his bed at around twenty-one yards. He never knew what hit him.

FARM PONDS, WATER HOLES, AND SEEPAGES

Although they do not generally need to go to water on a daily basis like some critters out west, whitetails will visit a clean farm pond or running creek if it is nearby. Indeed, a quick look at the water supply around your hunting grounds will probably turn up an abundance of deer tracks in the soft mud.

Several seasons ago I stumbled upon a seepage near the top of a steep mountain in a big woods area near my home in upstate New York. There were two or three pools of bubbling water in the seepage, and the wet ground nearby was just covered with deer tracks. Several old scrapes and rubs were also found in the immediate vicinity. I sat on a knoll overlooking the area for several evenings and soon learned that about twenty does and fawns bedded nearby. They visited the seepage on a regular basis, using it as a staging area of sorts before heading down the mountain to feed in the valley below. As near as I could tell, the only other water source was in that valley at least a half-mile distant.

When the rut kicked in, the area around the seepage was suddenly dotted with a plethora of fresh scrapes and large rubs. Bucks would visit the seepage to scent-check the does just like they would at a feeding site or bedding area. This big-woods water source turned out to be a veritable buck magnet.

To reach the seepage required a difficult climb, and I couldn't hunt it as often as I would have liked. Nonetheless, four of my friends hunted it off and on, and together we have tagged nearly a dozen whitetails there over the years. Now I make it a point to check out any clean water source tucked away in heavy cover that is situated near known concentrations of family groups of does and fawns. The water attracts the does, and during the rut the does attract the bucks.

CLEAR-CUTS

Hunting bucks in the wilderness is a supreme challenge. There are fewer deer per square mile, and to make your hunt all the more challenging there are no woodlots, cornfields, and other obvious food sources to help direct you to concentrations of bucks. There is one exception to this rule, however. Clear-cuts, especially those four to seven years old, are known to attract and hold deer in a big-woods setting.

The trick is to figure out preferred travel routes, those that afford easy access as well as those that promote security within the clear-cut. Your task will be greatly simplified once you begin to think of the clear-cut as nothing more than a big farm field. Suddenly, the corners and any low spots or nearby patches of thick cover will stand out as potential treestand sites.

My favorite clear-cuts are well off the beaten path, bordered by alder-lined creekbottoms, brush-choked ravines, and a good mix of softwoods and hardwoods. Bucks are attracted to this uneven topography and will often "walk the line" that separates those hardwoods from stands of mixed spruce and fir.

Four or five years ago while still-hunting in Manitoba, I caught a fat eight-pointer off guard as he moseyed through a clear-cut en route to a nearby swamp. In my view, there was really only one route a buck could take to reach that swamp, and that was along a finger of head-high brush that extended into the swamp. I'd like to tell you I nailed that buck, but he heard me and hightailed it back into the clear-cut like a scalded dog, never to be seen by me again.

Putting the squeeze play on a rutting buck is a good strategy, especially where two or more types of cover converge, such as a gentle slope leading to the head of a ravine.

One of the beauties of hunting clear-cuts is that does and fawns often do not have to leave the safety afforded by the leftover treetops and mounds of debris. That is, they can stay right inside the clear-cut where there is usually ample food, water, and cover. The trick here is to build a ground blind or erect a treestand near an entrance route. Or you can set up just inside the clear-cut along a creekbed or finger of brush and wait for an amorous buck to start poking around. Over the years I have caught several bucks flat-footed this way, including a 200-pound (field-dressed) six-pointer I shot at 100 yards as he entered the clear-cut via a creekbed.

FUNNELS

Putting the squeeze on a buck during the early season or pre-rut period is common practice, but when the rut goes into full swing, those funnels are usually of little consequence as bucks are now actively looking for estrus does, not food or shelter.

In wilderness settings, terrain features are more likely to dictate the path a buck will take to hook up with a doe in heat. His goal is to locate a willing doe while expending the least amount of energy, and one way he does this is by taking the "easy" route whenever possible.

Studying a topo map can help you locate these natural ambush sites before you ever set foot in the woods. Gentle slopes and spurs that lead up and down steep hillsides, for example, are natural routes for bucks to take. They may spend the early morning hours scouring the valley for estrus does and then head up the mountain along one of these routes to sniff-test probable doe bedding areas.

The brush-choked edges of pond, lake, swamp, or river are another big-woods funnel to pay close attention to. These are natural travel routes for bucks, and if you can get above that route and look down through the tangles you might just catch a big buck making his rounds. My friend Mark Eddy, a registered Adirondack deer guide, showed me such a spot several years ago that overlooked the edge of a thick swamp. Each fall the run was littered with fresh scrapes, and every year one of his clients got a crack at a rack working that scrape line.

The real killer funnels, however, are at the confluence of several terrain features. A gentle slope may lead down to a plateau that is bordered by a steep ravine. Bucks will be traveling along both edges of the ravine as well as going "around the horn" at the top of the ravine in their seemingly endless search for a doe in heat. The gentle slope will also steer bucks towards the top of the ravine.

Another funnel to look for exists on a saddle between two high peaks. These are really hot if the saddle also separates two swampy valleys or two doe bedding areas. The action here can be fast and furious when the rut nears its peak as bucks travel back and forth between bedding and feeding areas looking for estrus does.

THIN COVER

Every so often we hear about a first-year deer hunter banging a record-book buck from an out-of-the-way location, a place where no self-respecting "expert" would ever set foot because of the general absence of deer sign. But during the rut bucks will push hot does into these areas of sparse cover in an effort to keep the doe to themselves.

Often these love nests are not all that far from a morning food source frequented by family groups of does and fawns during the rut. Sometimes you will find such a spot situated on a finger of brush protruding from a creekbed, along a grassy fenceline, or even in a small, open woodlot bordering a cut cornfield.

Anytime you see bucks chasing does around is a good time to sneak and peak through these peripheral areas. Sooner or later you will catch a buck bedded with a hot doe along a downwind edge or next to some structure in the field such a rock pile or even a piece of abandoned farm machinery.

But the real reason to hunt these out of the way places of thin cover is the opportunity you have to bang a really big buck. After all, isn't that the main reason we all like to hunt the peak of the rut?

20

SOME LIKE IT HOT

by Patrick Durkin

Hot-weather rut hunts offer poor odds, but a low percentage is better than no percentage.

Most of us dread hot weather during deer season, especially when it stays through our best days to hunt rut-crazed bucks. Some hunters even avoid the deer woods when temperatures rise to unseasonable levels. I can't say they're wrong for doing so, especially if their hunting time is flexible. After all, daytime activity by mature bucks drops to almost zero during autumn heat waves.

But what about the rest of us? If we can only hunt weekends or vacation days or book a hunt for specific days with a nonrefundable down payment, we can't just wait for better days. We must make the best of a tough situation. It's never easy. Hunting the rut during hot weather ranks as one of deer hunting's biggest challenges. Not only must we deal with suppressed deer activity, we also must suppress our own negative attitudes about hunting in the heat. We fight nonstop urges to climb down early each morning, arrive late each afternoon, and avoid midday hunts altogether.

INCREASING THE ODDS

As most of us know all too well, North America has endured many hot-weather days during the rut in the past few years. Even so, some hunters find ways to increase their odds, however slight, of bagging big bucks while their fellow hunters spend more time complaining about the weather than doing something about it. Consider Wisconsin's Tom Indrebo, who operates Bluff Country Outfitters east of the Mississippi River in Buffalo County. Indrebo would prefer to wake up every day from late October through mid-November to overcast skies and frost-nipped earlobes, but no matter what the temperature, he must send paying clients out to their treestands. Indrebo kept asking himself what he could do to give hunters an honest hope of seeing a big buck, even when overnight temperatures stayed above forty-five degrees.

His solution? Water. Indrebo knew whitetails could survive without regular drinking. They can satisfy their liquid needs by eating crops, fruits, and browse. Then again, humans can survive without eating tenderloins, but who wants to exist on tofu? Indrebo reasoned that if bucks were running much of the night during hot weather to maintain their rutting obligations, they had to crave real water at some point. After all, their reproductive instincts allow little time for food of any kind, let alone those with high moisture content.

So where do bucks find water? Western Wisconsin has lots of creeks winding through its picturesque valleys, but hunting these water sources is often difficult, if not impossible. Even when hunters locate specific spots where whitetails usually drink, it's difficult to hunt the sites without alerting deer. Creeks, by their nature, run through tight valleys and narrow draws—terrain features that spawn swirling, unpredictable winds for treestand hunting. You might get away with an occasional valley sit, but fickle winds usually burn out such sites.

Indrebo considered those challenges and, confident that rut-driven bucks drink more water than most of us realize, decided the answer lay in landscaping. Farmers often create watering holes for cattle by bulldozing berms to plug draws at the edge of hilltop fields. Deer tracks pock the muddy shorelines of such ponds, but many of these sites aren't huntable, especially with a bow and arrow. They're usually in the open, and if they do have trees bordering them, the trunks are usually too small to hold a stand and their branches too sparse to conceal a hunter.

Although some hunters theorize that whitetails get all the water they need from the browse they eat, a hot-weather rut brings with it a whole new set of circumstances. Both bucks and does will frequent water holes during the chase phase.

GIVE THEM WHAT THEY WANT

Those cattle ponds gave Indrebo an idea, though. Why not hire someone with a bulldozer to create watering holes along the crests of his woodland hills? Ponds inside the woods would give bucks a water source they could use without exposing themselves in a field. Not only would the ponds be a magnet during the rut, especially during hot spells, they might attract deer for bowhunters in mid- to late September when temperatures stretch into the seventies and eighties. To make the ponds even more attractive, Indrebo planted clover in the surrounding bare dirt where the 'dozer carved out earth for the berms.

Indrebo's hunch was right. The ponds quickly generated consistent action. Some of them produce two or three Pope & Young bucks each fall. Although Indrebo usually places his treestands uphill within a twenty- to thirty-yard shot of a pond, his hunters usually shoot well before the bucks reach water. Here's why: After a berm plugs a draw and the pond fills up, deer soon trample trails through the brush and trees to reach the water. Indrebo finds those woodland trails, locates trees that overlook strategic sites, and installs his stands. When mature bucks approach a pond, they often pause near the edge of the clearing that borders it. Those long pauses are often their last.

Not all bucks follow the routine, of course. During a recent rut, one of Indrebo's clients hung up his bow at midday and started snacking on his lunch. Suddenly a buck crested the top of the pond's berm after walking up from below. The hunter put down his lunch and grabbed his bow as the buck approached the water and started drinking. Before the bowhunter could aim, the buck finished drinking, took two unhurried bounds, and disappeared back below the berm. Figuring he had nothing to lose, the bowhunter stayed up there the rest of the day, hoping the buck would get thirsty again. As evening neared, the buck again crested the berm, approached the water, and started drinking. Just as the Pope & Young buck turned to make its retreat, the hunter's arrow pierced its lungs.

TAKE TO THE GROUND

Another way to take advantage of a rutting buck's water needs is to act as if you're hunting pronghorns on the Great Plains. Many of us have grown so accustomed to treestand hunting that we have tunnel vision. We forget deer hunters as recently as thirty years ago did most of their hunting on foot or from ground blinds. Remember those farm ponds mentioned earlier? Rather than be stymied by a lack of trees to hang a stand, why not set up a commercial hay-bale blind or build a ground blind that resembles those large, round bales? The trick is to make them large enough to hide your form and to place two of them for different winds. Even then, don't hunt from them unless the wind is steady. These setups require close-up work and calm conditions or light, variable winds won't disguise the slight sounds you'll make when positioning for a shot.

In some situations—provided you own the land or have the owner's permission—you could even dig pit blinds. Most of us hear "pit blinds" and think of pronghorns or waterfowling, but earth blinds can work just as well for whitetails. In fact, I'd argue that because deer so seldom encounter anything resembling a pit blind, they're likely to be less aware of the potential for danger than with anything else we might try.

TAKE ADVANTAGE OF WINDS

Speaking of alternatives to treestands, it's possible to take advantage of high winds that often accompany hot autumn weather. This is a good time to stalk bedded bucks in uncut cornfields, windrows, and grasslands.

I'll never forget a recent Midwestern bowhunt when a friend and I arrived on October 24 to find mild temperatures. All week the air was warm and humid and long-sleeved T-shirts were the uniform of the day when we gathered in the pre-dawn darkness to discuss our plans. We were miserable and ornery. At midmorning one day, a truck pulled in with two bowhunters from the neighborhood. In the bed of the pickup lay a 150-class buck one of the guys had arrowed about an hour earlier. We assumed he was one of those lucky guys who just happened to have a buck walk within range, but we were wrong. He had stalked the buck after watching it bed in a weed- and brush-choked fencerow.

He told a good story. About two hours after dawn that day, he said he was as disgusted as the rest of us. He couldn't wait to get out of his treestand and head to town for breakfast. Just when he was

On hot days, rutting bucks bed before dawn or soon after. In farm country, watch for them to move into the riverbottom to bed in high grass and cool, sandy soils. (Photo courtesy of Bob McNally.)

ready to lower his gear, he spotted the buck moving down the fencerow a few hundred yards from his treestand. He watched through his binoculars as the buck stepped into a patch of brush and high grass, looked around, and lay down. The wind was gusting straight from the buck to the bowhunter, so he figured he had nothing to lose by trying a stalk. He marked the buck's bed with some reference points, lowered his gear, and descended. After reacquainting himself with the buck's bedding site from ground level, he sneaked to the end of the fencerow and began his stalk.

When he had crawled to within twenty-five yards without spooking the buck, he nocked an arrow, rose to one knee, and tried to find a shooting lane. The brush and grass blocked every possible angle. He dropped back down onto his haunches to rest and think. He decided the only way to get a shot would be to make the buck stand up. After rising again to one knee and drawing his compound, he gave a low whistle and increased the volume until the buck could hear it in the high winds. It finally stood to look around. Seconds later, the hunter's arrow sliced through its chest and out the far shoulder.

I know another hunter who regularly stalks rutting bucks in much the same way. The only difference is that he sets out each morning intending to stalk. He grew up near a Midwestern riverbottom that is now heavily farmed, and perhaps just as importantly, still populated by people he has known since childhood. He starts his day at dawn on high ground with binoculars and a spotting scope. On hot days, rutting bucks bed before or soon after dawn, and his trained eye spots them as they move into the riverbottom to bed in high grass and cool, sandy soils. Once a buck settles in, my friend studies the wind and terrain then makes his move.

These situations might sound unique, and maybe they are to some extent. What if your hunting is confined to one piece of land where ponds, fencerows, and uncut cornfields aren't an option? I guess I'd still rather stay in the woods during the rut than remove all hope by staying home. That being the case, if time is running short and the forecast calls for continued heat, you might need to go for broke.

When it's time to gamble, try setting up as close as possible to where a buck might be bedding inside a woodlot. In the morning, I want to be in my treestand and ready to launch an arrow at the first glimpse of legal shooting hours. Sometimes this requires an extra-early start and a long walk to avoid the buck's most likely approach routes. In the afternoon, I again arrive early and stay until legal shooting hours end. Chances are, if a buck comes through when temperatures are hot, it will be at the extreme edges of daylight, and it will likely be somewhere far back in from the edge of the woods.

Can rut hunts in hot temperatures be just as productive as hunts made on crisp November days when steam blasts from a buck's nostrils? Not likely. Then again, all it takes is one buck to make your hunt a success. Years from now, when you stop to tell the story behind the big buck in a photograph, few will care if you saw ten bucks that week or two. All they'll want to hear is how you got·him. And just think, you'll sound even more skilled if you can say you killed one of the only two bucks that made themselves vulnerable that day.

21

NEXT GENERATION DECOYS

by John Weiss

For some hunters, taking deer over decoys has become the ultimate rut-hunting technique. Add a little motion and you can make your setup even more realistic.

Sometimes we all like to take a little credit for being the first to accomplish something, no matter how inconsequential it may be in life's broader scheme. My own fifteen seconds of fame occurred more than ten years ago, and it involved, of all things, using a strip of toilet paper to put the mojo on an eight-point whitetail buck.

This was back when the decoys most hunters used were merely 3-D archery targets. Nevertheless, they're quite realistic, and when seen from a distance they quickly draw the notice of deer. But there was one particular buck, an impressive three-year-old, that refused to be fooled. He'd come to the edge of an oat field and stare at the decoy across the open ground, refusing to come even one step closer.

One day inspiration struck and I taped a short length of tissue paper to the decoy's rump so that it realistically flicked in the wind as a real deer's tail would do. When the buck arrived at the edge of the field the next day and saw the motion-imparting decoy, he literally raced toward the bogus deer. I killed that buck then and there.

The very next year provided more decoy excitement. An eight-point buck was directly beneath my stand. However, I couldn't shoot because the animal would not remain stationary. He was repeatedly goring a fawn decoy I had placed near a bedded doe decoy. The enraged buck would throw the fawn in the air with his antlers, circle it with head held low and neck hairs bristling, then gore and throw it still again.

Finally, convinced the fawn was dead, the buck rushed the bedded doe decoy and dug his antlers into her rump, trying to get her to stand so he could breed her. It was all to no avail and eventually he wandered off, never offering me a shot.

The two decoys were made by Feather-Flex, one of the most innovative companies in the field today.

"Forget that a fawn actually has no spots during the fall/winter hunting season," Feather-Flex's Dave Berkley had told me. "A buck doesn't think or reason that way. Like the males of many other species, all he instinctively knows to do is drive the offspring away from its mother and kill it so that he can get on with uninterrupted breeding activities.

"Another ruse with a fawn decoy," Berkley continued, "is tying it to a strand of fence wire and then running a fifty-foot length of fishing line to a nearby ground blind or treestand. By periodically jerking on the line, the decoy will jump and twitch as though

A doe-with-fawn decoy setup seems to enrage rutting bucks. They instinctively try to drive the fake offspring away from its mother, which is precisely what occurs when the rut hits. (Photo courtesy of Bill Vaznis.)

caught in the fence. To add realism to the theatrics, use a screaming fawn call, which reproduces the bawls and bleats of a distressed or injured deer."

This can be a dynamite tactic during the rut because it capitalizes upon a doe's maternal instinct to come to the aid of young of the species. If the doe is in estrus, a tending buck is sure to trail her right to your setup location.

UNDERSTANDING HOW DECOYS WORK

Other hunters who use decoys can undoubtedly describe the attraction to what is rapidly becoming the most exciting method of bowhunting whitetails. I've emphasized the word "bowhunting" because there is a consensus that using decoys during a firearms season, when the woodlands are crowded, would simply be too dangerous. Also, check your state's regulations regarding the legality of using decoys.

But why do deer respond to decoys in the first place? The most likely explanation is because deer simply like to keep company and interact with others of their kind. I've seen bucks and does alike rush into decoys and lick them, try to mate with them, and bed down among them. Yet since deer are so socially oriented, it's necessary for them to establish a very well-defined pecking order within their ranks. If this social ranking is violated, retribution of some sort is usually in the offing. In this regard, I've seen bucks and does also rush into decoys and kick them, bite them, horn them, or engage in a wide variety of bluffing and posturing.

However, whitetails are also very timid creatures that like to cling to the safety of dark shadows and dense cover. Within their personality framework there is a distinct paranoia that makes them quite hesitant to expose themselves in open places. But the weak chink in a whitetail's armor is that this fear is cancelled when a deer sees others already standing in an open place, whereupon it then feels compelled to join the party.

I've experienced many instances, primarily when watching open feeding areas such as meadows, in which deer approached the open edge from deep cover and just stood watching, apparently trying to assure themselves that all was right with the world. Yet when decoys are placed out in the open, deer commonly walk right out without hesitation. This is especially the case when a hunter is using decoys that are exhibiting a non-threatening motion such as a flicking tail or lowering its head to feed.

NEW MOTION-DECOY ADVANCES

In addition to practical innovations by hunters, decoy companies have been making strides forward themselves.

One of my favorite decoys of late is Delta's new At-Ease model. Weighing only seven pounds, it has an internal battery and motor, which causes its tail to gently swish from side to side. An adjustable program dial allows you to select any time interval from ten seconds to one minute between tail flicks. The value of this decoy break-through is that whitetails live in a world in which they're attuned to every movement within their visual range. They're attracted to some of the movements, are repelled by others, and engage in these move-ments themselves to communicate information to nearby deer. And over the years we've learned that when a deer's tail occasionally swishes from side to side, the animals are communicating content-ment and lack of fear.

If a hunter owns earlier-model decoys that don't have battery-operated motors that twitch tails, the Come-Alive Decoy Company makes an aftermarket "Tail-Wagger." This is a battery-operated, life-like tail that easily attaches to the rump of any deer decoy and can be programmed for eight- or sixteen-second wag intervals.

Two other popular decoys are actually lifelike, photo-imprint silhouettes of deer. Made of weatherproof fiberboard, they're sup-ported by upright rods pressed into the earth. One is the Higdon Motion Decoy and the other is the Outlaw. Both utilize an unbreak-able, ultra-thin Kevlar string that's laid out to the hunter's stand or blind. When the string is gently pulled, the Outlaw decoy's tail twitches back and forth. With the Higdon decoy, pulling on the string causes the tail to swish and the head to rise from a lowered feeding pose to an upright alert pose; release the string and the head lowers again, simulating a deer that has checked out its surround-ings and displayed the "all's well" body language.

THE RATTLING CONNECTION

Most decoys now on the market have easily removable antlers so the decoy can be used as either a buck or doe. Although buck and doe decoys can be used in a variety of ways, they are by far the most effective when a hunter rattles antlers or uses a grunt tube during the rutting season.

Also bear in mind that when a buck responds to the sound of antlers meshing in the distance, the animal expects to find one of two things. If he's the dominant buck in that neck of the woods, he expects to find two subordinate males jousting with each other and an estrus doe waiting nearby. In this case, he'll come in fast, making his hierarchal ranking known, drive the younger deer away, and then attempt to get cozy with the female.

Yet if the responding buck is a subordinate animal, he doesn't quite know what to make of the rattling and grunting sounds he hears in the distance. He may very well come upon two males that are even lower than he is on the totem pole, or he may find two superior animals attempting to sort out their differences. Consequently, he'll come in slowly and suspiciously, circling downwind and hanging back a safe distance until he has fully assessed the situation.

This is why hunters who rattle antlers and grunt often report entirely different responses from approaching bucks. Moreover, whitetails are adept at pinpointing the exact location of rattling and grunting sounds, and if they see no other deer at the scene upon their arrival they immediately become very suspicious and hang back or disappear completely. Therefore, a decoy provides the responding buck with the visual confirmation he needs to be lured in those final yards.

In fact, whenever possible, it's wise to use two or more decoys simultaneously. If you use only one decoy, and it just stands there staring in one direction, approaching deer may register alarm, but if you use multiple decoys and can simulate them interacting, the advantage suddenly swings in your favor. One way to do this, if you have two doe decoys, is to position them in a grooming pose to create a far more natural scene. The same is true for an alert doe decoy

Among other things, decoys divert an approaching deer's attention, providing the hunter with easier shooting opportunities.

standing next to a feeding doe decoy with her head down or a buck decoy standing near a bedded doe decoy.

BUCKS AND DOES TOGETHER

In going back to the subject of deciding whether to use a buck decoy or remove the antlers for a doe decoy, let the season and type of hunting you're engaging in dictate your choice.

For example, if my stand or blind is situated along the edge of an alfalfa meadow and the rut is not in progress, I'm waiting for deer to come to a favorite food source. And knowing in advance that they might wait until it's almost dark before stepping into the open, I'll place one or two doe decoys in the meadow.

The reason for this is because throughout the year whitetails live in a matriarchal society, and it's always the adult does, not the bucks, that are the decision-makers. As a result, among individuals constituting a band of deer, it is typically a mature doe that enters an open feeding area first and by her presence tells others still hanging back in their security cover that all is right with the world and it's safe to venture forth.

Doe decoys also are recommended during the peak of the rut when amorous bucks are tirelessly checking their scrapes. If a buck is hanging downwind to scent-check a scrape, a Delta At-Ease doe decoy right next to the scrape, with its swishing tail, may communicate to the buck "all's clear, come and get me."

You can also try using a bedded doe decoy situated in an open clearing, because a bedded doe communicates through her body language that she's a non-alert, relaxed deer and this instills confidence in a buck that sees the decoy. In addition, does that have just recently been bred commonly lie down in open areas because the bedding posture, with body-weight pressure exerted upon the lower abdominal area, helps to facilitate conception. Since a doe does not always conceive, this laying-down posture draws the interest of nearby bucks, which may be curious as to whether the doe in question will allow additional breeding to take place.

In most cases, however, I prefer to use a buck decoy during the rut because of the explosive excitement this often generates. I like to hunt in the vicinity of scrape lines or scrape clusters (as opposed to single, isolated scrapes), and to sweeten such scrapes with an estrus-doe lure.

FINE-TUNING YOUR TECHNIQUE

While the best location to station a doe decoy often is in an open clearing bordering a deeply forested region, the technique differs with buck decoys. I noted above that a hunter should be in the immediate vicinity of scrapes. But, more specifically, the hunter should use what has become known as the "cribbing" approach to determining the decoy's placement. This means putting the decoy directly in front of some type of barrier or obstacle such as bushes, brush, or perhaps a fallen tree.

This "blocking cover" prevents an approaching buck from coming in from behind the decoy, forcing him to circle around in front and presenting you the most desirable broadside or slightly quartering shot angle. If your stand is placed about thirty-five yards from the decoy, you should have a twenty or twenty-five yard shot at a responding buck that walks between you and your decoy.

In addition to bringing bucks into shooting range, whether by giving them a false sense of security so they'll step into open places or by alerting them to the presence of a ready doe or by challenging their hierarchal ranking, decoys have another equally important function. A decoy occupies an approaching deer's attention and thereby diverts it away from the hunter's location, which is extremely important when bowhunting animals at ranges close enough to count their eyelashes. There is far less chance of the deer visually detecting the presence of a human being in the immediate area or the slow movements he must make in getting his body into shooting position and then raising his bow.

In refining this technique, remember never to place a decoy directly facing your treestand or ground blind because a deer might turn to see what the decoy is looking at and see you. In the event that an incoming deer suddenly stops and begins stomping its front feet, or even snorting, don't worry. It's not your presence that is alarming him. He's simply trying to elicit some kind of response from the decoy, and eventually he will begin circling in an attempt to look it directly in the eye. So relax and enjoy the show until he provides the shot you want.

Also, consider using turkey decoys in conjunction with your deer decoys because the two species get along very well and often are seen feeding together along field edges and in forest clearings. My theory is that deer intuitively know turkeys are very shy animals with super-keen senses that prevent predators (man or otherwise) from getting too close to them. Consequently, deer seem to behave in a very relaxed manner when in the presence of turkeys.

Decoys provide an exciting new deer-hunting world, with a wealth of new tactics no one ever dreamed of ten years ago. Go for it.

22

TACKLE THE TRICKLE RUT

by John Weiss

*Nature usually orchestrates an orderly breeding season, but sometimes
she runs the show in spurts and stutters. Here's why and how to make
the best of a bad situation.*

During the 1996–1997 deer season I chased whitetails in six
states and in each place the local hunters groaned a familiar
lament. "We didn't have a rut this year! There were few rubs and
scrapes to be found, and the deer didn't respond to rattling and
grunting."

Yet as sure as dawn arrives after night, spring revealed another
crop of countless newborn fawns in those very regions, which is
proof enough that breeding the previous fall did indeed take place.

When a trickle rut hits, does and known food sources are the keys to finding bucks.

This was precisely what happened on my farm and lease lands in southeastern Ohio. It was early November, a time when bucks hereabouts usually are behaving like slobbering fools in their tireless search for estrus does. And yet, despite being in the right place at the right time, my pal Jeff Thomas and I had spent three days with our butts glued to the seats of our treestands and had seen absolutely nothing.

"Obviously, something is shutting down all deer activity," I shrugged as we began hiking back to the truck for a noontime lunch break. "I'm sure it must be the seventy-degree weather we're experiencing. By now we should have had several killer frosts and the average daily temperature should be forty degrees. My clover meadows should be brown and dormant by now, not lush and green."

Moments later, just as we approached a briar patch adjacent to a greenfield, deer exploded out of the cover and bounded away.

"I counted six," Tom said, breathlessly, "and one was a dandy buck."

Then the truly unexpected happened. With the deer now entirely out of sight, apparently having vamoosed for the next county, we continued toward our truck parked in the distance. Only seventy-five yards ahead we jumped the same group of deer again, with the very same big buck among them! For some strange reason, those particular deer just didn't want to be up and moving around, and after traveling only a short distance they wasted no time laying right back down. Maybe whatever was going on was affecting all deer in the area, which would explain why there were no deer sightings from our stands.

TIMING THE RUT

Before trying to explain the weird rutting seasons we sometimes experience, I'll briefly explain what happens when everything occurs the way it's supposed to. Under "normal" conditions, most bowhunters look upon the peak of the rutting period as the prime time to be afield because the heightened sexual anxiety of bucks often causes them to do goofy things. This is what makes them more vulnerable now than at any other time of year.

There are actually several distinct phases to the rut and the middle, or peak, period can be very difficult to hunt. At this time, nearly every buck is paired up with a near-estrus doe, engaging in what biologists refer to as a tending bond as they wait for the does to give the go signal. The moment breeding is concluded and conception takes place, bucks hurry off in search of other females.

Consequently, at this stage of the game, all bucks are single-minded of purpose. Their senses are focused almost exclusively on the does they are accompanying, and their travel patterns are thus determined by wherever the females may decide to go.

Admittedly, this peak-rut period is when a great many splendid deer are taken. But generally, it's because the bucks are on their feet and moving nearly all day long, and with their nostrils filled with doe-in-heat scent they commonly blunder into unsafe situations from which there is no escape. They make mistakes they wouldn't commit any other time of year, but this is unpredictable hunting because hunter success is far more likely to hinge upon blind luck rather than a well-executed plan.

Prior to all of this is the most action-packed rut-hunting phase of all, the pre-rut preparation period, which lasts approximately six weeks. Generally, this phase of the breeding period is from the last week of September through the first week in November in the northern half of the country; therefore, the hunting action is the sole province of bowhunters. But throughout the Deep South, the pre-rut may not begin until mid-November, with the peak of the rut taking place from late December to mid-January, which allows bowhunters and gun hunters to capitalize upon rut-hunting excitement.

To determine the probable onset of the pre-rut period in the region you live, ask a local wildlife biologist to tell you the date of the peak of the rut, then simply backdate by six weeks. In other words, if the peak of the rut in a given region is November 15, bucks will predictably begin engaging in pre-rut behavior about October 1.

WHEN THE RUT CHANGES GEAR

During either the pre-rut or peak-rut phases, Mother Nature quite often throws hunters a curve by drawing the curtain on all of the daytime mating activities deer engage in. Sudden and unseasonably warm weather moving into an area when bucks are just beginning to engage in making rubs and scrapes, sparring, and traveling widely in search of doe family units triggers this change.

We humans can add or remove clothing as the temperature changes, but deer are already wearing their heavy winter coats and growing fat stores to prepare for the worst that winter is likely to throw at them. Therefore, the sudden arrival of unseasonably warm weather makes them very uncomfortable and lethargic, causing them to just plain lay down and not move.

This retarded rutting activity often occurs simultaneously across many states. I remember hunting with RealTree's Bill Jordan just south of Atlanta several years ago during a rutting period that was unusually warm. In four days of sitting on stand all day, the six hunters in the group had not seen a single buck or doe. Finally, most of us played golf one afternoon while Bill got on his cell phone and began calling some of his hunting cronies in Alabama, Mississippi, Arkansas, and Missouri. They all said that in their respective regions they likewise were experiencing the worst rut-hunting season they could remember in years.

The best theory, according to biologists, is that deer instinctively know that engaging in strenuous, twenty-four-hour rutting activities during the unusually warm weather will result in such a high lactic acid buildup in their bodies that it can actually kill them. So what do they do? Well, they certainly don't cancel that season's rutting activity because that would be a violation of nature's code, over which they have no control, but they do alter the time frame in which the majority of breeding takes place each day.

I've since witnessed this in several states where it is legal to pan spotlights across open fields at night to locate deer. Predictably, when an unseasonable rise in air temperature shuts down daytime rutting activity, our "shining" endeavors reveal quite a lot of buck-chasing-doe activity between the hours of 11 P.M. and 5 A.M. Not surprisingly, the air temperature is often as much as fifteen or twenty degrees cooler at this time than during the midday hours.

Several things may tip off hunters that a trickle rut is in progress. Most noticeable, of course, will be the unseasonably warm weather, but it may also be unusually humid, damp, and rainy. Hunters will see little in the way of natural deer movements while sitting on stand. And grunt-calling and antler-rattling efforts, which should be red-hot at this time of year, will seem like nothing more than wasted energy.

FIND THE FOOD, FIND THE DEER

Taking a big buck under such adverse conditions requires first scouting suspected feeding areas, such as lush alfalfa meadows. Biologists who are attempting to understand this stop-and-go breeding phenomenon believe does and known food sources are the keys to finding bucks.

One study has shown that when a buck's testosterone level spikes upward in preparation for breeding, his thyroid gland simultaneously causes any previous desire to feed to cascade downward. Conversely, does continue to feed normally throughout the duration of their estrus cycles, and when the sudden warm temperatures cause a lull in the sexual activity levels of the animals, the does bed down very close to a known food source. In this manner, they need travel only very short distances—many times just a matter of yards—to satisfy their appetites with minimal exertion.

Bucks will predictably bed in close proximity to where the does are bedding. They, too, have an inclination to avoid overexertion in the face of the warm temperatures. Yet they want to be close to the females in order to monitor their estrus progress and to be able to quickly capitalize on any breeding opportunity when exactly the right moment arrives.

When I became privy to this new information, it suddenly became clear what had happened to Jeff Thomas and me on our Ohio hunt. We'd seen no deer activity from our stands because a lull had been triggered by a warm front pushing into our region. The does we jumped had been bedded in thick cover right next to the green-

A sudden cold snap during a trickle-rut breeding season will often get big bucks out and moving all day long.

field where they were intermittently feeding, and when they took off the lone buck in attendance followed along until the does once again bedded down.

Now that we were no longer clueless, we immediately pulled our stands overlooking scrapes and relocated two of them near clover meadows and two others near oak trees that weeks earlier had littered the ground with acorns. The following afternoon, Jeff arrowed a six-pointer as it stood in heavy cover watching nearby does gorge themselves in one of the clover fields. The buck briefly ran in a short circle and then fell in his own tracks. That same afternoon, on one of the acorn flats, I did a commendable job of sending an arrow a full six inches above the back of a small buck, but over the next two days I reclaimed my honor by taking two does.

REFINING YOUR STRATEGY

During a trickle rut, other feeding areas that may produce include croplands such as corn or soybeans, an orchard, a willow bar in a stream bottom, or any other prime food source deer locally favor. Just make sure it is a concentrated food supply, instead of sparse or widely scattered browse. And of critical importance, the food source must be situated closely to thick security cover that enables the deer to bed close to where they'll be feeding without having to travel more than 100 yards or so.

The next order of business is hiking entirely around the food source, looking for an abundance of tracks, but what you especially want to be on the lookout for are "doors." These are the entrance trails that filter into the feeding area from the bedding cover.

By following these trails back into the thick of things to learn where the deer are bedding you can easily dope out the best locations to ambush a buck on another day as he follows the does to and from their chosen food source.

Another cause of a stagnating rut in specific regions is heavy hunting pressure. This results in a marked reduction of the mature-buck age class, leaving the immature bucks to handle the bulk of breeding. Since immature bucks don't generate the same high testosterone levels as so-called trophy bucks, and therefore don't become as horny when does begin reaching the zenith of their estrus cycles, you simply don't see as much scraping, doe-chasing, and other ritualistic breeding behavior. Rather, the rut becomes a laid-back affair that occurs in spurts, stutters, and intermittent dead-stops.

So if it seems that there is a marked absence of scrapes, rubs, and other evidence of mating year after year with no explanatory heat spells, you can be pretty sure there is too much hunting pressure in your particular region and that it has resulted in a sex-ratio imbalance. Common sense should lead you to hunt elsewhere.

There are a couple of other things worth keeping in mind. The rut is more likely to go sour early in the hunting season during the pre-rut period when air temperatures are most prone to widely fluctuate, rather than later in the year when cold weather predominates.

Also, as a rule, the early-morning period, just an hour after dawn's first light, is the most productive time to hunt. This again goes back to the influence of the air temperature, which may not begin to decline appreciably until well after full dark. Conversely, until the morning sun fully clears the horizon, it stays cooler.

"The trickle rut is a splendid opportunity for a hunter to try to call a deer to his stand," says my friend Will Primos.

Will runs Primos Hunting Calls, and in addition to being one of the country's leading pioneers in deer-call research, he has produced a number of exciting videos revealing how deer respond to calls under a variety of conditions.

"When deer are lethargic during a trickle rut, calling too aggressively simply doesn't work," Primos explains. "So if you choose to rattle antlers or use a grunt call, tone it down. Make it an enticing, come-hither invitation rather than a bold challenge. Even better, try our fawn-bleat call. Does eagerly respond to the sound of a fawn in distress, no matter what the weather conditions. So if you can call in an estrus doe, any buck tending her will likely follow her to your location."

WHEN THE TIME IS RIGHT

A trickle rut usually varies in length according to the locale. In the Deep South, an unseasonably warm period may extend for a month or more. Yet in the north, a lull is predictably compact, and may be as brief as only a few days.

As a result, it's particularly important for hunters living in the north to have what I call a pre-scouted lull stand set up in advance of the season. In this manner, if a hunter is sitting on a stand overlooking a scrape line, for example, and the rut staggers to a halt, he can quickly shift his hunting efforts to a more productive stand location (near a feeding area) without wasting time scouting and unnecessarily spooking the animals in the area. All a hunter needs to do is quietly slip into his lull stand, knowing in advance that does and their attending bucks are nearby.

Once the lull is concluded days later, as a result of a new weather system pushing cold air into the region, the hunter should know to quickly abandon his lull stand and return to his former ambush sites over scrape lines.

Next time your rut is put on hold by unseasonably warm weather, temporarily forget about hunting the breeding areas and give yourself an edge; an "edge," that is, where heavy cover lays next to a food source that deer favor.

23

DRAW THE LINE ON SCRAPES

by Gary Clancy

Bucks rarely visit scrapes in daylight, but if you know when to be there
you'll find hunting scrapes is time well spent.

I guess I've spent more time than most men my age sitting in tree-stands waiting for deer to show up where I think they should show up. Many of those hours—weeks, really, if I totaled them up; heck, probably months—have been spent in stands overlooking scrapes. Yes, I've seen some bucks visit scrapes, and I've even killed a few as they pawed dirt or worked their antlers in overhanging branches.

But when brutally honest, I face this fact: When you factor in the number of hours spent hovering over scrapes against the number of buck sightings, the ratio is pathetic. It's so poor, in fact, that for

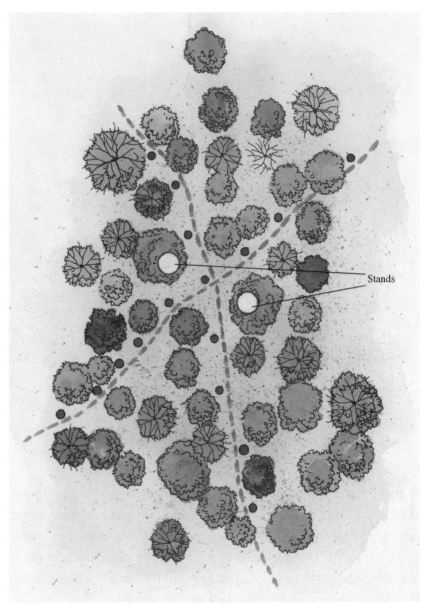

Laying fresh scent in an "X" pattern is a fine tactic during the chase phase.

a couple of seasons I quit hunting scrapes. I read a lot of research re-
ports on scrape visitations, and after realizing that eighty to ninety
percent of buck visits occurred in the dark, I had an excuse not to
hunt them.

But my scrape boycott didn't last. When hiking into my
evening stand on a little farm in western Wisconsin one day, I cut a
fresh scrape. I tried ignoring it, but I couldn't resist. After a little
snooping around, I found a string of five more scrapes marching
across the oak flat. This flat was egg-shaped and probably not much
bigger than a softball field, so five scrapes was a lot. And all of them
were big and fresh. Very fresh. I hung a stand in a twin-trunked bass-
wood tree between two of the scrapes and settled in.

By the time I climbed down three hours later, I had seen four
bucks work the scrape line. One was a scraggly little seven-pointer,
but the other three were good bucks, two eight-pointers and a ten-
pointer in the 120- to 130-inch range. The ten-pointer was maybe a
tad better. I drew on him when he squatted in the nearest scrape and
then, with my finger resting on the release trigger, I decided to wait.
I knew some real monsters lived in that area, and with all of the action I witnessed that afternoon, I just knew an even larger buck
would come along. As it turned out, I was wrong. But that's okay. I
had seen quite a show.

RETURN ENGAGEMENTS

I returned to that stand the next morning and stayed until dark.
I saw three of the same four bucks, but not the ten-pointer. I usually
don't hunt a stand three days in a row, but as far as I knew I hadn't
spooked any deer from this stand, and the scrapes were hot. So I
pulled another all-day sit the third day and was rewarded with four
buck sightings. Two were repeats, but the other two were newcom-
ers. One of them, the smallest of the four, made three visits that day.

The only mature buck of the four appeared a few minutes after the noon whistle blew in the town across the river.

I like hunting where noon whistles still announce lunch. In fact, I was digging a sandwich out of my pack when I heard the buck approaching. I instantly forgot about eating and slipped my Mathews from its hook. I hadn't yet seen the buck and didn't know if I would need the bow, but I've learned the hard way to get my bow in hand at the first hint of deer.

My first glimpse of the buck revved up my heart. He was steadily moving my way from a high ridge. Even from a distance, I could tell by the size and shape of his body that he was a mature buck. My first glimpse of antler sent my heart rate up another notch. The antler I glimpsed looked heavy. I slipped my release onto the string, adjusted my feet on the stand, did a quick once-over of my bow and arrow, and got ready for a shot. I judged that things would happen in a hurry. Like many mature bucks, this one wasn't taking the time to physically visit each scrape. Instead, he just cruised past downwind, letting his eyes and nose inform him of any interesting developments since his last visit.

Just before the buck momentarily disappeared into a stand of cedars, I sensed something was not right, but I couldn't determine what it was. When the buck reappeared, it hit me like a fist to the gut. The buck's offside beam was snapped off just above the brow tine. I had maybe three seconds to decide whether to shoot. Over the years, I've shot two half-rack bucks. In both cases, things happened so quickly I didn't realize it until I approached the dead deer. And in both cases I regretted killing them, so I let this big one-antlered buck cruise by.

WHEN TO HUNT SCRAPES

Action like that lured me back to scrape hunting, but even so, I don't spend as much time hunting scrapes as I once did. I now realize that timing is everything. The reason I nearly gave it up entirely was that I spent too many hours hunting scrapes at the wrong time, or I hunted the wrong scrapes at the right time. Let me explain.

For years, I hunted scrapes too late in the season. And after talking with hundreds of hunters who became disillusioned with scrape hunting, I believe the number-one reason for discontent is that hunters often stick with scrapes too late into the fall. Luckily, hunting near scrapes need not be a guessing game. As long as you hunt where the rut is relatively short-lived and intense, you can find the best times for scrape hunting by asking a deer specialist for local whitetail breeding dates.

For now, let's say November 10 to 20 is the peak-rut period. Many hunters mistakenly believe the rut's peak is a great time to sit over a scrape line. The truth is, it's a poor time to hunt scrapes. Bucks rarely visit scrapes while breeding is under way, and the few bucks that do visit are invariably frustrated youngsters who can't attract and hold a doe. The best time to hunt scrapes is during the weeks preceding the start of actual breeding. In a state where breeding peaks November 10 to 20, I concentrate my scrape hunts from mid-October through November 10, and I expect my best action from about October 27 through November 6.

Many hunters will probably be surprised at the November 6 date, assuming that scrape hunting would just get better as breeding activity nears. But bucks go into what's commonly called the "chase phase" of the rut about three to six days before breeding activities begin. During this hectic period, bucks are so frenzied that instead of patrolling scrape lines, they're running all over, chasing every doe they encounter. This is not a bad time to hunt scrapes, but there are places I'd rather be during the chase.

Although hunting over scrapes during the peak of breeding is usually a waste of time, there is sometimes a brief opportunity to shoot a big buck over a scrape on the rut's backside. When breeding

A big scrape like this is hard to resist, but unless it's part of a line of scrapes, don't hunt it. The author has found that lone scrapes, no matter how large, are rarely visited by bucks during shooting hours.

slackens, most bucks rest and eat to rebuild diminished fat and energy supplies. But the most dominant breeders, which are not always the biggest bucks, do not give up their sex drive so easily. Even though most does have been bred, dominant breeding bucks continue searching for stragglers to come into heat. These brutes remain on the prowl for several days after the rut peaks. During this time, they often open up a favorite scrape or two. I can think of worse places to hunt.

SELECTING TOP SCRAPES

If you have been frustrated in your scrape-hunting attempts, remember this: Rarely are the most obvious scrapes the best ones to hunt. In good whitetail country with a balanced herd, bucks scrape along the edges of every field and clear-cut in which does feed. These scrapes are easy to find and hunt over. The problem is that they're nearly all made and visited at night. Unless you're hunting a vast region with few hunters, field-edge scrapes are your worst investment in time. Scrapes in open, park-like timber aren't much better. Bucks, and especially mature bucks, aren't keen on strolling through "parks" during shooting light.

So, as you might guess, my main criterion for hunting a scrape is that it be located within fairly dense cover. I'm not talking about some tangle a cottontail rabbit couldn't navigate, but rather a habitat with enough cover to make a mature deer feel just secure enough that it might venture through during shooting light. When I find scrapes, the first thing I ask myself is this: If I were a big ol' buck, would I walk here in the soft glow of dusk or dawn to check these scrapes? If I answer no, I don't hunt there.

Location is one part of the puzzle. Numbers are another. In thirty years of sitting over scrapes, I have never found a lone scrape worth sitting over, and trust me, I've sat over a lot of them. I've seen lone scrapes the size of a hot tub. And I've seen lone scrapes that looked like they were rototilled by hard-pawing bucks. In fact, we once hung a surveillance camera over a lone scrape, and one 24-exposure roll of film revealed that twenty-one different bucks visited the scrape in one night. We hung a stand there the next morning, and I sat three days straight and saw three bucks. Not one was anywhere near the scrape. What happened? Lone scrapes are almost exclusively nighttime hangouts, and your odds of intercepting a buck there in daylight—no matter how big, torn up, or inviting it might appear—are slim to none.

I'll take a string of scrapes in or near heavy cover every time. A good scrape line sees more daytime action than does a big, single scrape. The closer one end of the scrape line is to a buck's bedding area, the better the scrape line will be. Why? Before turning in for the morning a buck is probably going to check those scrapes one more time. And one of the first things it will do after rising from its bed for a night of carousing is check nearby scrapes. For those who sit on a stand all day, it's not uncommon for a buck to sneak out of its bedding area at midday to check nearby scrapes while relieving itself, stretching, and working out the kinks.

A FEW TRICKS

I've also enjoyed some luck luring bucks from their bedding areas by grunting, doe-bleating, and rattling while in a stand over scrapes. Sometimes, too, I intercept bucks that just cruise by. And sometimes I use a decoy when hunting a scrape line. The main consideration is visibility. A decoy must be visible to deer from a distance. If a buck is right on top of a decoy before he sees it, the decoy will often spook him.

I always use scents when hunting over scrapes. When I hike into my stand I often drag a scent rag to lay a trail of doe-in-estrus scent to my stand. I even go out of my way to drag the rag through scrapes. Then I juice up the scrape or scrapes nearest my stand. If

I'm in a hurry, I might just squirt scent into the scrape as I pass, but more often I work scent into the scrape with a stick. If I plan to hunt the scrape line for a few days, I often bury one of those scent-impregnated Buc-Rut wafers an inch or two in the soil. This dirty trick encourages bucks to pay repeat visits. On overhanging branches, I hang a scent wafer or a wick saturated with forehead-gland scent.

And remember this: The overhanging branch is more important than the scrape. Many times I have watched bucks work an overhanging branch for minutes and pay little or no attention to the bare earth beneath their hoofs.

Maybe by now I've persuaded you to give scrape hunting another chance. Just accept the fact that at least eighty percent of all buck visits will be made at night. Sure, that's a bummer, but if my math is correct, that means twenty percent of the visits are made during shooting hours. In whitetail hunting, those aren't bad numbers.

This is especially true if you hunt the best scrapes at the right time of the season. Use rattling, grunting, doe-bleating, and deer scents to increase your odds. And then be patient. You won't see a buck checking its scrapes every time you sit on a stand along a scrape line, but when it happens, you instantly forget all of those long hours of waiting.

24

TEN STRATEGIES FOR RUTTING BUCKS

by Bill Winke

Changing hunting methods with changing buck behavior can also change your luck for the better.

Some of the most offbeat tactics can and will produce big bucks during the rut. With bucks traveling everywhere at this time, there are a lot of ways to be successful—and pure luck is certainly one of them. The bucks themselves don't even know where they'll be next; so how can you? But despite the seemingly random nature of the rut, there are a few things that are predictable, and by taking advantage of these you can help luck along and turn the odds in your favor. First, we need to find these threads of predictability. Not surprisingly, they depend on the specific phase of the rut.

Buck behavior changes as the rut progresses. Knowing which of the four phases of the rut you are hunting—pre-rut, pre-breeding, breeding, post-breeding—allows you to adjust your plan accordingly.

The following strategies are proven to produce fast action during all phases of the rut.

SCRAPE LINES

Phases: Pre-Rut and Pre-Breeding

There are two keys to successfully hunting a buck along his scrape line. First, you have to carefully find the sign. Too much scouting right now can educate a buck to the fact that he's being hunted. Smart old bucks pick this up quicker than younger bucks, so the type of animal you end up seeing may be a direct result of the way you scout.

Do most of your in-season scouting using an aerial photo while sitting at home on the couch. You should be able to predict where the travel routes and the scrape lines will be with fairly good accuracy. Now make a quick pass through the area and check out your hunches. This isn't the time to study every piece of sign (save that for after the season). Stay off deer trails as much as possible, and give known bedding areas a wide berth. You are looking for fresh scrapes located away from field edges. Thick cover is an added bonus. These sites offer the best hope of being visited by a good buck during daylight hours.

The second key to success is to pick the right scrapes to watch. Scrape lines (not individual scrapes) are your goal. They are, by definition, located along a buck's travel route. If the scrape that you are watching isn't along a believable travel route, the odds aren't good that a buck will come through. Set up in a location along the scrape-line travel route where you have a strategic advantage—where you can get in and out clean and where the wind works for you while on stand.

HUNT DOES DURING THE PEAK OF THE RUT

Phase: Breeding

Often you'll have to fool a doe before the buck that's following her offers a shot. A nice buck I took a few seasons back is a perfect example. The bruiser was following several does and fawns along a trail leading to an alfalfa field. All the antlerless deer had to pass downwind of me before the buck got to my shooting lane. I held my breath as first one and then another sauntered down the trail totally unaware of my presence. Finally, they all made it past and I could breathe a sigh of relief. I was glad I had hung the stand high. I made good on the twenty-five-yard shot and was soon admiring the heavy-antlered eight-pointer. I was hunting along a feeding area, but it wasn't the food that attracted the buck; it was the does.

Does are religious about using trails, so almost any well-traveled path has the potential to produce big-buck action at this time of year. Try to find a place where two trails cross, either close to a feeding area or between two bedding areas. When the rut peaks, you simply can't go wrong hunting this pattern. But remember that although the bucks are nomadic at this time, the does aren't. You have to be able to consistently fool the local does, or they'll move off—taking your chances with them. Don't over-hunt any stand.

BOTTLENECKS FOR TRAVELING BUCKS

Phases: Pre-Breeding, Breeding, and Post-Breeding

You can't beat a good bottleneck during most phases of the rut. Anytime you can find a seam in the terrain or a strip of cover that offers both concealment and the path of least resistance, you have struck the mother lode. Typically, you'll find scrape lines through most of these places, but don't count on sign to give them away. Use your imagination.

Bottlenecks are great places to intercept rutting bucks. Finding a good rub line early in the season will tip you off to the most popular travel corridors.

Terrain-related funnels include such features as saddles, steep bluffs, and river crossings, to name only a few. Cover-related funnels can include brushy fencelines, narrow fingers of cover, and the inside corners of open fields that extend into thick timber. Be on the lookout for these and many other natural bottlenecks in the areas where you hunt. When bucks are on the move, these spots are dynamite.

WATCH AND LEARN

Phases: Pre-Rut and Post-Breeding

My favorite game plan, especially when hunting a new area, is to take a stand where I can both hunt and watch for visual signs of buck movement. I call it hunting from the outside in—learning as I go. I'll choose a vantage point such as a brushy fenceline or wooded ridgetop as my starting point. It takes patience not to rush right in and hunt the hottest buck sign in the area, but you'll be rewarded by keeping the pressure off until you know just how to proceed to the next step. After only a couple of stand sessions you should have seen enough to plan your attack.

Though hunting from observation stands is one of the most effective and overlooked strategies, it won't work everywhere. If your hunting area gets a lot of pressure, it is unlikely that bucks will show themselves where you can see them during daylight hours. If you feel this is the case where you hunt, this strategy will only lead to boredom and frustration. It would be better to look for the thickest patch of brush you can find for your stand.

THE TIME AND PLACE TO CALL

Phases: Pre-Rut, Pre-Breeding, and Post-Breeding

The right setup is an important part of successful calling. It is tough to draw deer into an area with wide-open understory. They're not dumb; instead of coming to investigate, they'll simply stand back and look. Thick cover around the calling site will greatly improve your odds of pulling a buck close.

Because a wary old buck will first try to circle downwind before coming to a call, you should keep an open field, river, lake, or steep bluff close on your downwind side. This will prevent the buck from winding you before you get a chance to at least see him. Though he may stop without offering a shot, that buck won't stop using the area like he would if he scented you.

Everyone has an opinion on the best rattling and grunting technique, and for the most part, all of them work. From my experience, technique is far less important than timing and location. Remember, regardless of how hard you try, you'll never be able to duplicate the sound of a real buck fight, anyway.

When calling from a stand, short sequences spaced out every half-hour throughout the day are about right. In the pre-rut, mix grunting with light rattling; save the heavy clashing and grinding for later.

THE ULTIMATE MORNING STAND

Phases: Late Pre-Breeding and Breeding

One morning a couple of seasons back I experienced the most excitement I've ever had on stand. Three different hot does ran past, each being followed closely by several bucks. The action took place well back in the timber on the edge of a doe bedding area during the middle of the morning. As soon as I see bucks begin to chase does, these are the spots I reserve for my morning hunts. Bucks will start showing up shortly after sunrise and will mill in and out of the area all morning as they hunt for an estrus doe. Does will start out using these areas heavily just prior to breeding, but as the amount of chasing increases they will tend to spread out to avoid the commotion. However, the bucks will continue to come through looking for them.

The tricky part about hunting bedding areas is managing your impact. You can't afford to educate the does, or they will stop using the area prematurely and so will the bucks. Keep your stand to the downwind fringe of the bedding area in a place where you can get in and out without being seen, heard, or smelled. You'll find that this eliminates a lot of potential stand sites.

WHEN TO HUNT FEEDING AREAS

Phases: Pre-Rut, Pre-Breeding, and (early) Breeding

Feeding areas are a lot like bedding areas. They start to produce excellent results when the bucks start chasing does. Although bedding areas are great spots for morning stands, feeding areas are best hunted in the afternoons. Does will use their customary feeding areas heavily until the bucks get to hounding them so badly that they start avoiding these areas. This typically doesn't happen until the middle of the rut's breeding phase.

Set up along the main trails heading into the feeding area, but stay within range of the edge trail that runs about forty yards inside the wood line. Bucks will often cruise this edge trail to intersect trails leading in and out of the feeding area while sniffing for signs of an estrus doe. It is also good, whenever possible, to cover the outer edge of the cover from the same stand. Bucks will also cruise along the edge of the timber where they can cut trails and visually watch for does.

OBEY THE CARDINAL RULE

Phases: All rut phases

No matter what strategy you are using or what rut phase you are hunting, there is one cardinal rule that should supersede all other thinking: *You'll never tag a buck that knows he's being hunted.* Even though the bucks are on the move a lot during most rut phases, you still have to hunt carefully so that you don't tip your hand.

For example, if you are careless in approaching your stand and flush the does from a bedding area, they will go stomping, crashing,

A careless approach to your stand may push a buck out of your hunting area completely. Obey the rules for scent control at all times.

and snorting through the timber, severely reducing your chances for success from that stand that day. Even if you bump a deer that slinks out of the area without your realizing it, other deer will tell by its body language that danger is near. The disturbance will hang in the air, and natural movement will be reduced in that area for several hours.

Of course, every bowhunter knows he has to play the wind when on stand, but few realize the importance of also playing the wind when approaching and exiting a stand. Getting in and out cleanly is the real challenge you must meet to take a trophy buck. The hunters that master it become the ten percent that consistently take ninety percent of the trophy bucks.

BE AGGRESSIVE WHEN YOU CAN

Phases: Pre-Breeding and Breeding

Early in the rut—in the pre-rut phase—bucks are just starting to increase movement as a result of rising testosterone levels and are still staying close to home. At these times you can't be a bull in a china shop or you'll be discovered and the jig will be up. However, as the rut advances, bucks become more and more nomadic. You'll see bucks you've never seen before and will never see again. Now you can increase your impact without much fear of burning out your hunting area—but only if you are hunting certain types of stands.

Obviously, you can't afford to educate all the does, so you can't get too aggressive near bedding and feeding areas. But you can put in more time in areas that are frequented only by bucks. The classic example is a travel funnel located between two doe bedding areas. Bucks will move through this corridor at all times of the day. Don't worry if you get picked off by a few bucks. They likely would not have been in the area in a day or two anyway. New bucks that don't know anything about your hunting patterns will be moving through regularly.

If you have a favorite stand that is located well away from doe concentration areas, you can hunt it repeatedly at this time of year (as long as the wind is right and you can get in without being detected).

MORNING OR EVENING?

Phases: All rut phases

Mornings are better than evenings. This is my conclusion after many years of hardcore rut hunting. Bucks seem to move longer into the morning than they do in the afternoon. Generally, I can count on about two hours of movement in the evenings and about four hours of movement in the mornings. Morning hunts double my chances of getting a shot. I think bucks are more exhausted in the mornings, and they are prone to make mistakes and walk more—a combination I don't mind using to my advantage. Of course, you have to be in the right places to see this kind of activity, but I've already covered my top picks for morning and evening hunting.

Hunt as much as you can, but if you're forced to choose between giving up a morning hunt or an evening hunt, give up the evening hunt every time.

For most hunters, the rut is the best time of the season. It is when they take their vacations and when they hunt their favorite stands. To be most successful during this time frame you need a game plan that changes with buck behavior. Take advantage of their weaknesses during each phase of the rut, and you won't have to count on pure luck.

25

BUCK CLICKING— THE NEW RAGE

by Bill Vaznis

Some have called it the ultimate breeding call for whitetail deer.
Others call it pure dynamite in the woods.

The situation was explosive. I was still-hunting along a brush- and weed-choked power line in northern Missouri when I heard a loud crash about 100 yards distant. A small doe emerged from the far side, wheeled about, and bolted toward me with her tail held high and off to one side. She was obviously in heat, and as I scanned the brush behind her I caught several glimpses of a huge-bodied deer with a tall, wide rack in hot pursuit.

The buck did not break cover, but nonetheless followed the doe's progress, stopping behind a wall of thorns just twenty-five yards away. The doe stood motionless in front of me with her head down and hind legs askew, while the buck snorted and "clicked" in the brush. She was in heat all right, and her bleating made her needs sound quite urgent. The buck seemed frustrated at the long wait, and emitted a series of sharp clicks followed by a loud snort-wheeze. I didn't know it at the time, but there were two record-class bucks in pursuit of that hot doe, and the larger was of Boone & Crockett proportions.

I'd like to tell you I arrowed one of those deer, but the truth is I blew a shot at the smaller animal without knowing the 170-class behemoth was also in attendance. I also misread the scenario, thinking the two distinct clicking sequences followed by a snort-wheeze came from the same buck. I know better now.

There is no doubt that buck clicking is an awesome sound. Unfortunately, like the grunts of a trailing buck, buck clicking often goes unnoticed in the deer woods. I suspect this is because most hunters simply do not recognize the clicks as having anything to do

Stay alert. Although it is one of the loudest deer vocalizations, buck clicking often goes unnoticed by hunters focused on drawing bucks in by rattling.

with deer or deer hunting. Indeed, a long series of evenly spaced clicks sound more like a kid dragging his thumb along the teeth of a plastic comb than part of the courtship ritual of a mature and sexually-experienced buck during the peak of the rut.

But that is exactly what the series of staccato-like clicks represent. According to Adirondack deer hunter Dave Oathout, creator of Legend Lures and the first person to publicly recognize buck clicking as a form of whitetail communication, a buck vocalizes his maturity and the fact that he is sexually experienced to the opposite sex just prior to mating. And he does this by inhaling air to create a four- or five-second series of loud, evenly spaced clicks.

Oathout grew up on a whitetail deer preserve owned by his father. About eight years ago he purchased a video camera to film and study whitetail behavior on the preserve and an adjacent 11,000 acres of private wilderness in upstate New York. It didn't take long for him to categorize various whitetail vocalizations, and in the process unravel one of the most pervasive secrets of the mating ritual.

"First of all, a doe smells right for three days, but is only willing to stand and be bred during a short twenty-four-hour period," explains Oathout. "If a doe is not yet ready to breed, but is nonetheless harassed by an amorous buck, she will often simply lay down in an effort to thwart his sexual advances. A young and inexperienced buck might charge in anyway, using his rack to get her to stand up and be bred, and inadvertently goring her.

"By contrast, a mature buck will do everything he can to pass on his genes. One of the ways he does this is by communicating to a doe in heat that he is indeed a mature, sexually experienced buck— a prime specimen. And he does this by first emitting a contact grunt and then clicking, which in effect tells the doe that 'I am a mature buck and I know the mating rituals. I am not going to hurt you, and I will not be overanxious. I will remain calm and wait until you are ready to mate.'

"This is what I call the true tending grunt," says Oathout. "On the other hand, a young buck or even an older buck with limited sexual experience will simply start walking toward a potentially receptive doe, hoping she will stand still and be bred. As of yet I have not seen an adolescent buck initiate the process with a contact grunt—a true sign of a mature buck. Nonetheless, when he gets to within fifteen yards or so he will begin clicking his intentions to her. If she is ready and willing to be bred, she will get into a submissive posture.

"More often than not, however, he will not exhibit the right body language, and being in a rush to mate for the first or second time in his life, will become overanxious and start to hyperventilate. That is, he will click by inhaling *and* exhaling air. Don't forget, he is full of testosterone and anxious to pass on his genes before another buck enters the scene.

"If the doe is mature and sexually experienced herself, she may just flee, knowing that the buck approaching her is neither mature nor sexually experienced. She may even sense he may harm her in the process.

"A mature buck will emit of a series of clicks, then wait three or four minutes for the doe to get in position. Keep in mind that he is pumped up with testosterone himself, so much so that he is sick to his stomach and has very little interest in eating. If she will not stand to be bred, he could get a little impatient. Indeed, even though he is trying to maintain his composure, his next series of clicks will be a little more intense. The doe however will not stand to be bred until her hormonal levels tell her it is time. This may be too much to ask for even a mature buck; he will increase the tempo of his clicking again, ending with an electrifying snort-wheeze signifying to the doe that he is a dominant animal and that he is getting very impatient."

Hunter freshens a scrape, prior to rattling and 'clicking'.

BUCK-CLICKING STRATEGIES

The best times to try your hand at buck clicking are during the late pre-rut and throughout the peak of the rut, when bucks are actually on the prowl looking for a doe in heat. Its effectiveness wanes as the rut winds down.

Start out by clicking slowly, and then quicken the pace by inhaling and exhaling to simulate a hyperventilating yearling buck. If you are in a treestand, add some realism by moving from left to right or right to left in a wide arc to make the target buck think the young upstart is pushing the doe too hard.

Another option is to position buck and doe decoys in the open near your stand. The buck decoy should be standing over the doe and sporting a small to average rack. You want him to look like a yearling buck so that any passing mature bucks will not only realize that he is probably sexually inexperienced, but also not be put off by his size. In other words, the target buck believes he can come rushing onto the scene and take charge of the hot doe with impunity.

I used an interesting strategy last fall while still-hunting near my home in upstate New York. One morning I came upon two yearling bucks in hot pursuit of an estrus doe. She was leading them on a merry chase through the woods and open fields. It was obvious she was not yet ready to stand and allow herself to be bred. As she zigzagged about, it was not uncommon for one or both panting bucks to lose sight of her. All it took for one of the bucks to pick up the trail again was a snapping branch, a buck grunt, a series of buck clicking, or a doe bleat. I chose to imitate the grunt of a young buck, and, sure enough, one of the "lost" bucks came running to me believing I was on the trail of the estrus doe. I took my best shot, but, alas, I missed him cleanly.

26

FIFTY WAYS TO CALL THE RUT

by John Weiss

There are dozens of deer calls on the market. These all-time best tips will make every one of them more effective.

1. Too many hunters who use grunt calls try to sound like the biggest and baddest buck in the woods. This only serves to intimidate and scare away most bucks. Tone down your effort so you sound like a wimp, and you'll draw a greater response from bucks that think they can whip you.
2. If you see a deer in the distance respond to your call and begin coming your way, put the call down. It has performed its job. If you keep calling you'll only increase the chances that the buck will pinpoint your location.

3. An estrus-doe bleat call is perfect for the peak of the rut. When a doe is in full heat she goes looking for a buck. She periodically stops and bleats, then looks around and listens for a response. This particular call sounds almost like a standard grunt call, but rather than being continuous, it is comprised of one-second bleats between three-second pauses.

4. When deer are slowly feeding through thick cover and frequently out of sight of each other, they use a contact call to remain aware of each other's location. When you mimic this call, the key to an authentic sound is making it rise and fall in pitch.

5. A hunter's success in using rattling antlers to bring in a buck hinges on doing the rattling either on level ground or high ground. No one knows why, but deer seldom respond to rattling if it means having to travel downhill into bottomland.

6. When on stand, always pay careful attention to any deer around you. If one of them begins staring in a particular direction and makes a contact call, it is aware of still other deer you can't yet see. A buck may be about to step into view, so don't even blink.

7. Most call manufacturers have cassette tapes available so you can listen to how the calls are supposed to sound and then practice them before going afield. But don't worry about being perfect; just like humans, deer have slightly different voices.

8. Few hunters are aware of it, but there is one type of call that actually is intended for use during deer drives. It's the deer-whistle call, which makes a shrill sound that quite often will cause a fast-running deer to stop dead in his tracks, giving a nearby hunter a brief moment in which to take careful aim at a stationary animal.

9. If you don't like to have numerous calls hanging around your neck while on stand, consider one that has a reversible reed, which produces two different levels of volume and pitch. Or consider a call with various O-ring settings within the reed or a

call in which the reed can be adjusted by means of an exterior push button; both types offer a wide range of volume and pitch. For unknown reasons, one particular tone works better than others on some days.

10. When you are ready to begin your first antler-rattling sequence, don't begin too loudly or aggressively. There may be an unseen buck very close to you, and he may perceive you to be a boss buck and run away. It is better to start off rattling softly, and if nothing comes to you, gradually increase the volume and intensity.

11. The fawn-bleat call is rapidly growing in popularity as a way to call does during the rut. Why call does? Because a doe's maternal instinct causes her to respond to what she perceives is a fawn in trouble. During the rut, a buck tending an estrus doe will not leave her side to respond to any call. But if you call in the doe, the buck is sure to follow her right to your location.

12. The effectiveness of a fawn-bleat call depends on its realism. If you've ever heard a fawn caught in a fence or being pulled down by a coyote, it screams its lungs out. So really put on some theatrics with your call and it will be more effective.

13. When bowhunting and wearing a mesh face net, it's not necessary to raise the bottom of the net to place your mouth on the end of the call. Simply blow right through the netting as though it wasn't even there.

14. When bowhunting, teaming up with a partner makes calling and antler rattling doubly effective. Place the "shooter" in a treestand and out in front of the "caller" by forty yards. When a deer responds to the calling effort, it will usually walk right under the lead hunter as it draws closer to the source of the call, providing an easy shot.

15. Is it really necessary to master the use of so many different calls now being made by manufacturers? Yes, because biologists at the University of Georgia, using tape recorders, identified

fifteen distinctly different vocalizations made by whitetails. The more "deer talk" you can mimic, the more successful you'll be in your deer-calling efforts.

16. Previously, grunt calls emitted only one tonal pitch at one volume level. Now many have ribbed tubes that can be extended from four to eight inches to produce various pitches and degrees of loudness. As a rule, use the higher pitch and higher volume to get a deer's attention from far away, then reduce the pitch and volume as the deer comes closer. The higher volume also is more effective when windy weather prevents the sound from carrying very far.

17. Always use a grunt-snort call in conjunction with antler rattling because using one without the other isn't a genuine sound when bucks interact during the rut.

18. Throughout the year, deer are not continuously vocalizing with each other, so don't overdo it with prolonged calling. The exception to the rule is during the rut, when deer vocalizations of various types are far more frequent; go ahead and call every five or ten minutes throughout the day during this period.

19. Blind calling (with no animal in sight) can be effective, but calling to a deer you can see in the distance works better.

20. When using any kind of call, don't expect an immediate response from a deer that hears it. Although this happens sometimes, quite often a deer will stare for a long period of time, trying to first make visual confirmation that another deer is near before venturing closer.

21. When rattling antlers, always pay close attention to your immediate right and left, and especially directly behind you. Quite often a responding buck won't come straight to you from the direction you expect but will circle to come in downwind.

22. We all need to cough or clear our throats on stand. To do this without sounding distinctly human, muffle your mouth against

When rattling, pay attention to your immediate left and right, and directly behind you.

your jacket sleeve and try to simulate a grunt call. Then quickly follow up by blowing on a real grunt call. A nearby deer that hears your throat-clearing noise and the genuine grunt call immediately after won't be as alarmed as when you just cough in the usual manner.

23. A predator call, such as the screaming rabbit, should be part of every deer hunter's arsenal. Its usefulness was discovered in Texas when coyote hunters found more deer responding to their rabbit calls than coyotes. Biologists believe a deer's response to a predator call is based purely upon curiosity.

24. If there's a curved, ribbed tube on the call you're using, it has a definite purpose. You don't have to turn your body to blow your call in a different direction and thus make a movement that deer may detect. Instead, just bend the ribbed tube in the direction you want to "throw" the call. This reduces a deer's ability to focus on your exact location.

25. Many bowhunters prefer a hands-free call to help bring a deer in those last few crucial feet while they are in the process of raising the bow and drawing the string.

26. An alternative to cumbersome rattling antlers is a rattling bag or rattling box. With a bit of practice you can produce buck-fighting sounds that closely duplicate the real thing.

27. When evening darkness arrives and the day's hunt is over, many hunters don't know what to do if there is a deer close by that they don't want to shoot. Don't simply begin climbing down, which will likely spook the deer. Instead, begin barking like a dog. The deer will leave, but it won't associate the event with human activity in the area.

28. Contrary to what most hunters think, the best time to use a grunt call and rattling antlers is not the peak of the rut. By then, nearly all bucks are paired-up with estrus does. The best time to use a

grunt call and rattling antlers is the two-week period before the rut begins, when bucks are alone and looking for action.

29. If you want to grunt during the rut, use one of the new calls that allow you to both inhale and exhale. This mimics the breathless excitation of the tending grunt bucks make when scent-trailing a doe in heat. If a buck hears this and is between does, he may respond in the hope of horning in on another buck's intended mating activity.

30. During any calling effort, your eyes are crucially important to the outcome. Deer have an uncanny way of slipping in close without making a sound or exposing themselves in openings. Continually take the cover apart in all directions around you for the slightest glimpse of a wary buck putting the sneak on you.

If you don't want to have numerous calls around your neck, consider a push-button call, which will help keep your movements to a minimum when an alert buck is in the neighborhood.

31. Many hunters like to saw the brow tines off their rattling antlers and use a grinding wheel to smooth down the bumps on the antler bases. This surgery will prevent your hands from taking a beating when you aggressively rattle, and it doesn't affect the tonal quality of the antlers.

32. If a buck responds to your call, comes in, and then detects your presence and snorts and bounds away, he's not likely to return to that same exact location for a long time. If you want to have another chance at him, it's imperative that you relocate your stand at least 200 yards away.

33. During the pre-rut, be a triple threat by simultaneously using a grunt call, rattling antlers, and decoy. But for safety's sake, use this technique only during the bowhunting season.

34. Throughout the year, does are far more vocal and socially oriented than bucks. So don't be disappointed or surprised if a majority of the animals that respond to your calls are females.

35. If you call in a buck that hangs up out of shooting range and won't come any closer, do nothing. Stop calling and allow him to turn and slowly begin walking away until he's almost out of sight. Then call again. Frequently, the buck will wheel around and race in closer.

36. When using a grunt call, the most effective sequence is usually three brief two-second grunts with a two-second pause between each one.

37. In bitter cold weather, moisture from your breath may eventually cause the reed in any deer call to freeze up. Preventing this is easy. Simply lower your jacket zipper a few inches and slip the call inside when not using it.

38. When attempting to call deer, you're performing theatre and the more realism you can convey the more successful you'll be. This is one reason why the use of scents makes any calling effort more effective.

39. There is no truth to the myth that large-sized rattling antlers will call in the biggest bucks, but it is true that bleached or dried-out rattling antlers don't yield the same authentic rattling sounds as fresh antlers.

40. If hunting pressure is usually intense in your region, you'll see the best success if you call during the middle of the week when fewer hunters are prowling around. Restrict your efforts to the heaviest cover you can find.

41. Early in the fall, when bucks are sparring, don't loudly clash your antlers together or you'll scare them away. Just lightly tickle the antlers to make a sound like a flamenco dancer clicking castanets. The time to loudly clash your antlers is later during the pre-rut when bucks are aggressively fighting.

42. If you see a buck trailing a doe and they travel out of sight without responding to your call, keep calling. If the doe isn't in estrus, the buck may lose interest in her and eventually turn and come back in your direction.

43. When attempting to rattle in deer from ground level, don't be too anxious to leave and try another place if a buck doesn't immediately respond. Particularly on a still day when there is no wind, a buck may hear your rattling from half a mile away, and it may take him twenty minutes to slowly sneak in your direction.

44. If a small buck responds to your call, don't be too anxious to take him until you are sure that he's not being followed by a much larger deer that is about to step into view.

45. When bowhunting, wrap your call with camo tape so its shiny plastic housing won't glare in bright sunlight.

46. If there's a second rut in your area, it will peak twenty-eight days after the peak of the first rut. So about two weeks after the peak of the first rut, which is the pre-second-rut period, begin grunting and antler rattling again. And once the second rut is underway, again use your tending-grunt call and fawn bleater.

47. For any call to work, deer must be able to hear it. So always concentrate your calling effort in those locations where deer are most likely to be at certain times. Call around feeding areas early in the morning and just before dusk. Midday, call near bedding thickets. During the rutting period, call in the vicinity of scrapes and rub lines.

48. When rattling, add more realism to your antler-meshing performance by stomping on the ground with your boots and raking the antlers against brush to simulate the various sounds bucks make when fighting.

49. Don't expect deer to respond to your calling efforts every day. Only the deer can explain why, but sometimes numerous animals will come to your calls one day and then none will respond the very next day.

50. Don't ever call when a deer is looking straight in your direction. He'll surely peg your exact location and may also spot you moving. Call again only when the deer looks away. Keep him guessing, and he may eventually walk right beneath your stand.

27

BAD-WEATHER RUTTERS

by Peter Fiduccia

When weather during the rut turns wet, snowy, or just plain frigid,
your rut-hunting tactics might need an overhaul.

The doorbell rang just as I placed another log in the fire-place.

"The door's open, Felix. Come on in," I said as the hot-burning embers instantly ignited the bark of the new log.

"Guess you've decided it's raining too hard to go deer hunting," Felix responded.

"No. Quite the contrary," I said. "We're going. I just want a good warm fire to dry us off and warm us up when we get back."

I could see by the expression on Felix's face that he thought I was either kidding or trying to be macho. He couldn't believe that I was about to take him to the "Buck Tree" in a torrential rainstorm. While driving to the stand, he kept reminding me that deer aren't supposed to move while it's raining—even during the rut—especially in downpours.

I glanced at him and, with as serious a face as I could muster, said, "If you want to shoot your first racked buck, don't worry about the rain, just post by the Buck Tree today. I don't think you'll be there too long before you see the buck I've been telling you about."

DEER DO MOVE IN THE RAIN

All too often I hear deer hunters complain that deer don't move in driving rain. Nothing could be further from the truth. Deer regularly move about to feed or breed during inclement weather—especially in the rain. I've actually seen more deer than normal moving in the snow and rain. The trick to hunting successfully during rough weather is persistence, patience, stamina, and comfort. Without these basic components, foul-weather hunting is an exercise in futility.

Deer hunting is a great challenge, and although there are proven foul-weather hunting strategies, there are equally important strategies for the hunter to consider before he even steps from the truck and into the woods. These non-hunting strategies are the foundation for foul-weather hunting success. Ignore them, and no hunting strategy that I can offer you will work to its potential.

To be a successful foul-weather deer hunter, first motivate yourself to go hunting on a rainy day—even during a serious rainstorm. Without this determination, the battle is lost before it has begun.

Once you have convinced yourself to hunt in this type of weather, you must be prepared to stay on stand as long as you would if you were hunting on a clear day. Hunting in foul weather demands this type of patience. It will regularly pay big dividends, though, especially during the rut, when anything can happen at any time.

Severe wind is perhaps the greatest obstacle to poor-weather deer hunting. When the wind blows hard, bucks will sometimes hole up and it's up to you to get in after them.

CLOTHING

Foul-weather deer hunting requires some special preparation and planning. But by thinking ahead and employing some unusual tactics you can brave all but the most hostile weather and come out successful. You'll increase your days afield and your chances of taking a trophy buck. If you're prepared for the worst, you can remain comfortable and stay in the woods long after other hunters have given up and headed back to camp.

Dressing in layers and taking quiet raingear, a dry change of clothes, and hand warmers are the most important points to remember. Over the years, I've found that wool clothing offers great protection from the elements, as well as being quiet. I like to use it over a layer of long underwear. On top of the wool, wear a rainproof jacket and pants. A high-quality set of Gore-Tex raingear will last for years and is worth the investment. Be sure to buy an outfit a full size larger than your regular clothing so that it will fit without binding. It's also important to wear the right hat (one that diverts rain away from your eyes and the back of your neck), gloves, and socks.

When you are armed with quality clothing, you have put your first strategy into play. You will be able to remain on stand much longer, no matter what the weather conditions are. And the longer you are on stand, the more you increase your chances of seeing and taking a buck.

FOOTWEAR

The next strategy—one that is just as important as your clothing—is keeping your feet dry and warm. Waiting for, or stalking, a buck in the rain or snow can be miserable if your feet are wet and cold. There is no compromising on this matter. A quality pair of warm, waterproof boots is an absolute necessity.

EQUIPMENT

While you are protecting yourself against the elements, don't forget to protect your equipment, as well. If you're using optics, binoculars, or scopes, make sure they are of good quality, with a flip-up cover (or something similar) to keep the lenses dry and clear. Also, carry a soft, absorbent cloth to occasionally wipe down the scope. If you're using a rifle in freezing weather, be sure you've disassembled the bolt and degreased it, because bolts can, and do, freeze in weather as warm as twenty degrees Fahrenheit. Reassemble the bolt and lubricate it only sparingly with a lightweight gun oil. Heavy grease may cause the bolt to freeze solid or to strike the primer so lightly that it won't ignite the round.

It's also a good idea to put a light coating of car wax on the barrel. It makes rain and snow slide off just like it does on the hood of your car or truck. This helps protect the barrel from dampness and rust and allows you to keep your mind focused on the activity at hand—hunting! Use a wax that has as little odor as possible.

Once you learn how successful you can be when hunting during foul weather, you may eventually want to purchase an all-weather rifle with a synthetic stock.

FOOD

Another strategy that pays for itself over and over again is never to go afield in foul weather without a thermos of hot liquid (soup or broth) and some solid food. Nothing drags you out of the woods faster than a hungry stomach or a chill that cuts to the bone. It's amazing how a thermos of hot soup and some food can turn a miserable day into one that's tolerable.

DEER AND BAD WEATHER

Now that you are warm and dry, let's examine some of the unusual traits that rutting whitetail deer may exhibit in foul weather and how to use these to your advantage.

In all but the most extreme weather conditions (two-day snowstorms, gale-force winds, ice storms, or torrential rainstorms that dump three inches of water in a twelve-hour period), deer generally are unable to remain bedded when the weather turns nasty—at least not for long anyway. They instinctively know that they must feed despite the conditions. In fact, these conditions give the edge back to the hunter. I have used gusty winds to sneak up undetected on bucks bedded in laurel, on ledges, or nervously feeding in woodlots or fields.

During high winds, a deer's senses are dramatically reduced; this is why they become so nervous. Unfortunately for them, they still must find food, especially during a prolonged period of windy days. By using the wind to conceal your scent, noise, and, to some degree, the sight of your approach (with everything in the woods blowing in the wind, it's harder for deer to detect your movement), you can often sneak up on a deer that would have picked you off during normal weather conditions.

During snowstorms—besides being able to quietly track deer into their bedding and feeding locations—you can position yourself on known trails. Deer often move along trails to feed or chase does and bed down again despite the snow. Waiting along these trails during a continuing snowstorm pays off handsomely.

Bad weather can also push deer into moving at odd times of the day. While they are normally nocturnal, whitetails may spend a large part of the day moving before or after a storm. This activity often intensifies as the storm begins or just after it has ended. Dramatic changes in temperature or barometric pressure have been proven to motivate deer into movement before, during, and after a storm. This is especially true if bad weather has forced them to be stationary for an extended period of time.

Stand and still-hunting remain the best tactics for foul-weather deer hunting, but with one serious twist. Instead of a little movement here or there, it will be feast or famine. If the deer are moving, they will move continually. If they're not traveling, however, it will take additional effort, like stalking, to get up on them. Learning how to recognize the varying conditions that govern these different patterns is the key to deciding which hunting technique you should employ.

If the wind is above thirty-eight miles per hour and a storm has been in the area more than a few hours, chances are the deer will be "holed up" and will stay that way until the storm breaks or their hunger becomes so great that they are forced to look for food. The still-hunting can be awesome during these conditions. Hunt any and all places that afford secure cover to deer. In this type of weather, they won't be bedded where they normally would be. Instead, they will seek out the densest cover they can find, usually a stand of evergreens or thick lau-

Periods of poor weather will not curtail the rutting urge of whitetail bucks. Deer may bed down for a short while, but will generally be on the move during the rut. Motivating yourself to get out in it is tougher than the hunting.

rels void of hardwood trees with snapping branches. I can't stress enough that you need to take your time and go slowly. Still-hunting in standing corn during conditions like this also can be an excellent strategy. Deer, especially big bucks, often head for standing corn swales and other timber-free hiding places during heavy winds and rain.

Other variables to consider besides prevailing weather conditions include food availability, time of year, and the stage of the rut. The closer it is to full rut, the greater the chances that bucks will be moving regardless of harsh conditions. The bucks will either be with does, which will be holed up, or out seeking an estrus doe. This means incorporating a more typical rut-hunting strategy into your foul-weather plan. Use an estrus scent (like Love Potion No. 9) in a drip dispenser or on the bottom of a boot pad as you are walking to your stand. Often, a buck on the move will pick up the scent and move into your area. During heavy rain, I often hang a boot pad saturated with estrus scent in three or four different locations to help attract any bucks on the move. It is the only time I hang more than one boot pad and use excess scent. Rain suppresses the odor, so you need to use more scent and pads for the strategy to be effective.

Another factor to take into consideration during bad weather is the distance at which you'll be shooting and your shot placement. At best, your vision will be at least slightly impaired. At worst, it can be cut by more than half. With this in mind, shorten up your self-imposed maximum shooting distance. Also, be particularly careful about your shot placement. In rain or heavy snowfall any sign will be more difficult to read even minutes after it is made. In the case of heavy rain, sign may be obliterated immediately.

These conditions make bowhunting especially difficult. I rarely bowhunt in the rain unless I am already on stand with a buck within range when the rain begins. If you decide to bowhunt in the rain due to the good hunting rainy conditions can offer, follow up quickly on all shots. For instance, a deer that has been arrowed in the heart or lungs can still run 100 yards or more. In a torrential rainstorm, most, if not all, blood sign could be eliminated—resulting in a lost deer even though you made the perfect shot. To help reduce the chances of this happening, reduce your range by half and only shoot when you think your arrow placement will be perfect.

Due to the elimination of sign during foul weather you should start tracking within five minutes. Yes, you stand a chance of spooking a wounded animal and causing it to run farther after it's hit, but you also stand a much better chance of finding the animal than you would without the help of visible sign.

Remember that weather conditions like relative humidity, air temperature, wind, snow depth, precipitation, barometric pressure, cloud cover, and moon phase all play important roles in deer behavior and movement. Learn what effect each specific weather condition has on deer movement and you will be a much better hunter—in good weather and bad.

A good attractor scent can tip the odds in your favor during bad weather.

Generally speaking, only the most intense weather dramatically changes deer movement. A snow depth of eighteen inches or more immediately puts deer into "yarding" behavior, and they will congregate in softwood wintering areas. Gale-force winds—when large tree branches are snapping and entire trees are bending or being uprooted—send deer into thickets and the most protected cover they can find. Rainstorms that drop several inches of rain in a few short hours also deter deer from moving. Extremely frigid conditions over extended periods put deer down, too.

But whitetail deer will continue to move during foul weather that isn't so intense. They are not really physically affected by foul weather; it doesn't bother them enough to curtail movement. Remember this, and you may put a big buck on the wall and meat in the freezer during the next foul-weather day you encounter. Take Felix for example.

Felix discovered how good foul-weather hunting could be on the day I was talking about earlier. I placed him by the Buck Tree at 3:15 P.M. and told him where I thought the buck would come from and when. In fact, I explained to him that the buck regularly traveled through the area around 4:15 P.M. I also cautioned him that because of the heavy rain, the buck might come through earlier.

As Felix settled in, I walked to my own spot roughly 100 yards away. I was just tying my gun to the string to hoist it into my treestand when I heard the shot. When I got to Felix, all he could say was, "I can't believe how casually this buck was walking and feeding on acorns in such a heavy rainstorm. He never knew I was twenty-five yards from him when I shot him."

Felix's eight-point buck had an eighteen-inch spread and dressed out at 160 pounds. For his first racked whitetail, it was a dandy—and he took it on a lousy, rainy day when most hunters stayed home.